MEDIATIZED POLITICAL CAMPAIGNS

MEDIATIZED POLITICAL CAMPAIGNS

A Caribbean Perspective

Indrani Bachan-Persad

THE UNIVERSITY OF THE WEST INDIES PRESS
Jamaica • Barbados • Trinidad and Tobago

The University of the West Indies Press
7A Gibraltar Hall Road, Mona
Kingston 7, Jamaica
www.uwipress.com

A catalogue record of this book is available from the
National Library of Jamaica.

ISBN: 978-976-640-618-9 (print)
978-976-640-619-6 (Kindle)
978-976-640-620-2 (ePub)

Cover design by Richard Mark Rawlins
Book design by Robert Harris
Set in Minion Pro 10.5/14.2 x 27
Printed in the United States of America

I dedicate this book to my family, especially my daughter,
Kielash Chelsea Persad, with the hope that she too will be
inspired to pursue her dreams and become a published author someday.

Contents

Figures

Tables

Preface

THE ROLE PLAYED BY THE MEDIA IN POLITICAL campaigns in Trinidad and Tobago has been one of the most understudied areas by scholars in the country. This book examines the interplay between press and politics in political campaigns during a period of electoral volatility in Trinidad and Tobago, in which five elections were called in the ten years from 2000 to 2010. In this fairly young democracy, elections were called at a rate of one election every two years within the period studied. Elections are due once every five years. This book explores whether the manner in which newspapers in Trinidad and Tobago framed their political coverage of the national elections inevitably conveyed bias towards political parties, giving them an edge over their competitors in the run-up to national elections. The objective of this book is to share a better understanding of the relations between press and politics and identify possible solutions to strengthen both the independent role of the media and the democratic process in a small island state such as Trinidad and Tobago. Further, it makes a case for a new model of media and politics based on the developing status of small countries, building on existing models.

Significance of the Period under Study (2000–2010)

To the discerning eye, there was something amiss within the realms of media and politics in Trinidad and Tobago, given that five elections were held during these ten years. Questions about the appropriateness of the political system and election cycle under the current constitution and the need for constitutional reform have been raised. Indeed, the need for constitutional reform seems to persist in the national agenda, in spite of review of the 1962 independence constitution and the establishment of a republican constitution in 1976.

The period under review was one of steadily deteriorating relations between certain media owners and professionals in the journalistic field on the one hand and politicians on the other, especially prime ministers of the country. Relations between the press and politicians deteriorated during the campaign periods, especially during the lead-up to elections, with prime ministers openly accusing the media of biased political coverage and of having partisan affiliations with certain politicians and parties. Evidence points to the local press becoming increasingly influential in the political communication process, and to it even maybe being instrumental in the early calling of an election in 2001, 2002 and 2010. Taken to its logical extreme, the press may even have triggered the fall of two prime ministers who had dominated politics for more than the decade of politics under review in this book.

The press may also have paved the way for the emergence of a new permutation of the political-party system and a different approach to governance from the traditional two-party system, which was dominated by the People's National Movement (PNM) and the United National Congress (UNC). In 2010, for instance, a coalition party emerged comprising several political parties, such as the Congress of the People and a number of other smaller political parties, under the umbrella of the People's Partnership.

Relations between the Press and Politicians

Relations between the media and political parties have always been interspersed with moments of drama in Trinidad and Tobago, but within the recent past, especially since 1995, such relations have been especially contentious. The facts would indicate that both political parties (UNC and PNM), while in power, have used the state to curb press freedom whenever they thought the press was especially critical of their government. Basdeo Panday, leader of the UNC, became the first East Indian prime minister of Trinidad and Tobago and the only prime minister from a political party with absolutely no connection with the PNM, which had dominated politics since pre-independence and self-government in 1956. A.N.R. Robinson, who became prime minister in 1986 under the National Alliance for Reconstruction government, had served in various high offices in party politics and PNM administrations from 1958 to 1970. Panday had from the beginning been an opposition politician, emerging as a leader of forces opposed to the PNM since its founding. From 1995 to 2000, Panday had a running row with the *Guardian*, which led to the managing director being asked to resign and several editors and journalists also left in a mass walkout. In 2001, Panday complained about unfair treatment by a media house he said was vindictive towards his administration and had an ethnic agenda aligned to the interest of the PNM.

Before 1995, however, when Panday became prime minister for the first time, relations between the press and the PNM government had also soured considerably during the 1991–1995 period, when the PNM governed the country. Between 1994 and 1995, the press was generally very critical of Patrick Manning's style of leadership as head of the PNM government. The media were very critical of Manning's action to place the speaker of the house, Occah Seepaul, under house arrest; of the firing by fax of the minister of foreign affairs; and of the sidelining and eventual firing of Manning's minister of trade, Brian Kuei Tung, over allegations he had leaked the election date to the opposition UNC before the election.

By 2010, in a later administration, when Prime Minister Patrick Manning called an election prematurely for 24 May, there was a fully combative and hostile relationship between the PNM administration and the press. During the 2010 campaign, the government publicly accused the media of biased reporting against the PNM government, with Prime Minister Manning accusing the daily press of being anti-government.

The opposition forces of the People's Partnership capitalized on the open hostility between the PNM and the media by championing the cause of the media during its 2010 campaign. At that time, Kamla Persad-Bissessar had earned considerable goodwill from the media by the way she conducted a clean campaign, among other things, during the UNC's internal party election. In addition, she received considerable sympathy from large sections of the population for the barrage of attacks, personal and otherwise, from her political colleagues within the UNC as she contested the leadership position, challenging the founder and political leader of the party, Basdeo Panday.

As a result, she received extensive coverage from the media, which catapulted her to national celebrity status and positioned her to become the leader of the UNC and opposition leader, as well as the first female prime minister of the country.

The 2010 election was also one of those rare occasions in which race was not a dominant factor in the coverage of national elections, and to a significant degree, this was reflected in voting behaviour in the actual election in 2010. Politicians have traditionally exploited the race factor to win elections because the two largest ethnic groups, East Indians and Africans, almost equally made up the population, with East Indians comprising 35.4 per cent and Africans 34.2 per cent (Central Statistical Office 2011). Further, the Westminster system, as part of the British colonial legacy and modified by the colonial British government, facilitated a majoritan system based on a two-party system of governance. This inevitably resulted in the two dominant political parties, the PNM and the UNC (or its predecessors; notably, the Democratic Labour Party and the United Labour Front), being composed of Africans and East Indians respectively, so that the two main parties were linked to ethnic appeal. However, in 2010, national politics seemed to have transcended race politics, and voting appeared to have been based on the need for good governance by the most promising candidates and party.

It was also the first time in the evolution of national politics that gender became a dominant theme during national elections, with a woman, Kamla Persad-Bissessar, emerging in the male-dominated profession of politics both to lead a political party and to become the first female prime minister of the country. Her ascendency represented a change in party politics in terms of structure, leadership and governance style, while placing gender at the centre stage in politics and shattering preconceived views of the role of women in politics, governance and society.

The Complexity of Analysing Elections in Trinidad and Tobago

To understand the complexity of the relationship between media and politics in Trinidad and Tobago, this book is primarily (although not exclusively) concerned with framing theory (Cappella and Jamieson 1997; Iyengar 1991; McCombs 2004; and Price et al. 1997), based on the observation made by theorist Robert Entman (1991) in his study of the US news treatment of two plane crashes that the manner in which global events are covered and presented can influence a dominant perception. Implicit in this observation was the element of biased media coverage. For my own purposes, I examined bias from the perspective of balanced and objective reporting (Cenite et al. 2008; Garyantes 2006), using Westerstahl's (1983, 419) concept of balance in terms of the amount of negative and positive coverage given to political parties during elections. However, as the complexity in the relationship between press and politics became more apparent, other theories were drawn on, such as media effects theory (McQuail 2008), agenda-setting theory (Cohen 1983; Entman 2004;

Lang and Lang 1981) and postcolonialism and democratic theories (Curran 1991; Voltmer 2007), to critically appraise the dynamic of media and politics in Trinidad and Tobago.

This book includes case studies of five electoral campaigns based on analysis of a large body of press clippings from the three local daily papers: the *Guardian, Express* and *Newsday*. Further, interviews were conducted with select media practitioners, and these facilitated valuable insights into the journalistic profession as practised in the country and gave me an appreciation of the challenges faced by those involved in this field.

Evidence based on the empirical research points to the press not only having a strong effect on electoral outcomes through the manner in which it framed particular parties, politicians and issues but also maybe having actually precipitated the early calling of elections before they were constitutionally due. This was especially true of those prime ministers who were openly hostile to the media and in situations where press/politics relations had become combative, as found with the Panday (2000–2002) and Manning (2007–2010) regimes.

Scope of the Book

The book, although limited to Trinidad and Tobago, a small country in the Caribbean of approximately 1.3 million people, does draw extensively from media and political systems in other democracies worldwide. This book takes into account the stage of development of the free press, resulting from deregulation by the state in 1986, as well as the availability of material to support research. Many Caribbean territories have not reached far in the development of their media systems. These states are generally small, and the media are still very much under state control. The challenge of the cross-cutting ethnic dimension also presents its own complexities.

New Model of Media and Politics

This book makes a case for a new model of media and politics: an emerging liberal-democratic model, or an adjustment made to the liberal model created by Hallin and Mancini in 2004. This proposed model takes into account the developing status of small countries such as Trinidad and Tobago, which have small media systems, in which the media have enjoyed considerable freedom and generally been allowed to flourish under the democratic system, but are constrained by a sense of social responsibility that plays a developmental role in the democratic process as such a country moves forward on a development trajectory.

Plan of the Book

The book comprises eight chapters. The empirical research on the five elections focused on three separate case studies, with one case study being done of the first campaign period during the 2000 election and another of the 2010 campaign period at the end of the period. The two parameters allowed for comparative study from the start to the end of the research period. The other three elections, 2001, 2002 and 2007, were done as one case study with a view to comparison within a single chapter. The three chapters, covering five elections, would constitute the empirical basis on which to draw conclusions. Chapter 7 embarked on a comparative analysis of the five elections based on the three empirical chapters to determine trends in electoral coverage of political campaigns while engaging in a discussion based on the research questions and objectives, with a view to charting a way forward for media and politics. The final chapter charts a way forward for media and politics in Trinidad and Tobago, with implications for other similar countries. Two historical chapters were also completed to give a broader understanding of the role of the media as it existed in the pre-independence era from 1956 to 2010, when the last election covered in this book was held. It becomes clear that allegations of media bias by prime ministers of Trinidad and Tobago, starting with the first prime minister as premier, Dr Eric Williams, in 1956, have always been a feature of national life. As a result, examination of the empirical data is located within a context of a history of adversarial relationships among prime ministers, ruling parties and the press, in which accusations of media bias have been a feature.

The title of the book points to the growing role and influence of the media in Caribbean politics as mediatization evolves as a major phenomenon in politics all over the world. Mediatization is a word created to describe the extent to which multimedia messaging has become a central feature of political campaign strategy. Within this context, the role of the press in the context of a general mediatization of campaigns becomes fundamentally important. The term media as used in this book has been used interchangeably to mean the press, namely, the three daily newspapers: the *Express*, *Newsday* and the *Guardian*.

Acknowledgements

WHEN I STUMBLED UPON COVENTRY UNIVERSITY DURING A routine institutional visit, I never once thought of pursuing my doctoral studies there, much less developing my research into a book. I have had the most wonderful experience there as a mature student, and for this I thank the university for offering me a home away from home.

I wish to sincerely thank a number of people at both Coventry University and the University of the West Indies who have truly believed in me and supported me through this academic journey: my mentor, Bhoendradatt Tewarie, who supervised my research and provided overall support for me to complete my PhD while working full-time at the University of the West Indies, and my director of studies at Coventry University, Fred Okoth Mudhai, who pushed me very hard from the very first day and kept me on track while focusing on the finish line. Thanks also to my academic support at Coventry University: Andree Woodcock, Gary Hall, Sean Hides, and support staff at the International Office, Sarah Spiers and Andy McNicol.

I also wish to thank my family, especially my husband, Kassinath Persad; my daughter, Chelsea; and my mother, Poptee Bachan, all of whom were my backbone during my studies abroad. Also, my sisters Rhona, Angela and Carol; sisters-in-law Maria Mahabir and Tara Moonesar; brothers and brothers-in-law and nieces and nephews, all of whom never stopped believing in me.

Thanks also to the staff at the Institute of Critical Thinking: Gillian Siu and Crispin Gomez and research assistants Jahana Copilah and Giselle Garcia. I also wish to thank my sponsors: the University of the West Indies and Global SantaFe (through my sister Carol) for partial funding towards my research. I also thank those journalists and editors from the three newspapers who have graciously participated in the survey on journalistic practices in Trinidad and Tobago: Sunity Maharaj-Best, Raffique Shah, Tony Fraser, Ira Mathur, Andy Johnson, Ken Ali, Wesley Gibbings, Clint Chan Tack and Kevin Baldeosingh.

Abbreviations

CCN	Caribbean Communications Network
COP	Congress of the People
EBC	Elections and Boundaries Commission
MORI	Market and Opinion Research International
NAR	National Alliance for Reconstruction
PNM	People's National Movement
PP	People's Partnership
TOP	Tobago Organisation of the People
TTT	Trinidad and Tobago Television
UNC	United National Congress
UDeCOTT	Urban Development Corporation of Trinidad and Tobago

CHAPTER 1

Media and Political Systems

THE RELATIONSHIP BETWEEN MEDIA AND POLITICS IN DEMOCRACIES worldwide is complex and varies from country to country because of country-specific issues such as the nature of the society, cultural norms and traditions, type of political system and state of media development, as well as history and geographic location. This is even truer in a newly democratic, small society such as Trinidad and Tobago, emerging out of a history of colonialism and state-dominated media into a freer deregulated media environment facilitated by the constitution of the country, in which freedom of the press is enshrined.

This complexity is explored in five general election campaigns in Trinidad and Tobago over a period of ten years, from 2000 to 2010, in which the role of the media and their influences on the outcome of these elections during a volatile political period in the country's history were examined. At a rate of one election every two years, even though elections are constitutionally due once every five years, the rapid changeover of governments during this period and the role of the media in the political communication process, together with their influences in the calling of early elections, demonstrate the growing importance of the media in developing a healthy democracy. Whether that role has been compromised by framing elections to influence electoral processes and outcomes, and to ensure good governance in the interests of the citizenry of the country through biased political coverage, is debatable and will be explored fully in this book.

To understand Trinidad and Tobago's society, there must be a deeper under-standing of the historical context of postcolonial societies struggling to become fully autonomous and independent while developing their own identity. New democracies such as Trinidad and Tobago, which grew out of post-independence, one-party rule, inherited a unique set of problems that shape the relationship between the media and government: namely, a strong state, which saw itself as a protector of development and had a curious relationship with its colonial past. Further, in many countries with deep ethnic and religious divisions, "nation building is still an unfinished project so that social integration and national unity appear as primary values above individual liberties and open debate" (Voltmer 2007, 248).

The Political Landscape of Trinidad and Tobago

Trinidad and Tobago was a colony of Britain from 1797 to 1962. It became an independent state with a governor-general in 1962, and in 1976, it became a republic with a non-executive president and a Westminster-style parliamentary democracy. The constitution of Trinidad and Tobago recognizes a parliamentary democracy, with a prime minister as head of government, an attorney general essential to the cabinet, an independent judiciary and free media in a secular state that holds parliamentary elections every five years. It would be reasonable to claim that the constitution of Trinidad and Tobago provides for the operation of a liberal democracy. However, between 1956, when Trinidad and Tobago achieved self-government (the country was granted independence in 1962), and the 2010 election, Trinidad and Tobago was governed by a single party, the People's National Movement (PNM), excepting three five-year terms, between 1986 and 1991, when the National Alliance for Reconstruction (NAR) defeated the PNM; 1995–2000, when the United National Congress (UNC) formed the government (although it received another term, it was only able to govern for two of the five years); and 2010–2015, after the People's Partnership (PP) emerged victorious at the polls.

Although the country has had a history of a two-party political system with smaller parties emerging from time to time, in reality, the country has had a hegemonic party system dominated by a single party, the PNM, from 1956 to 1981 (Barrow-Giles and Joseph 2006). Coalition parties only emerged in efforts to remove the long-standing PNM government from office, when the NAR and the PP formed the government (in 1986 and 2010, respectively).

Also, in 1995, when the election had resulted in a tie of seventeen to seventeen, with the NAR gaining two seats in Tobago, a coalition was formed between the UNC and the NAR to form the government. However, although

Table 1. Trinidad and Tobago: Electoral Outcomes and Party Fortunes, 1956–1991

Year and Party	Number of Parliamentary Representatives	% National Vote	Total Number of Votes Cast	% Electoral Turnout
1956				
PNM	13	38.70	271,534	80.10
PDP	5	20.30		
Other parties	6	31.30		
Independents				
1961				
PNM	20	57.00	333,512	88.10
DLP	10	41.70		
1966				
PNM	24	52.40	302,548	65.80
DLP	12	34.00		
1971				
PNM	36	84.10	118,597	33.10
1976				
PNM	24	54.20	315,809	55.80
ULF/UNC	10	27.20		
Other parties	2	18.60		
Independents				
1981				
PNM	26	52.60	415,416	56.40
ULF/UNC	8	15.20		
Other parties	2	31.80		
Independents				
1986				
PNM	3	31.10	577,300	65.40
NAR	33	67.30		
1991				
PNM	21	45.10	522,472	65.76
ULF/UNC	13	29.10		
NAR	2	28.90		
1995				
PNM	17	48.76	530,311	63.30
UNC	17	47.22		
NAR	2	4.76		

Source: Elections and Boundaries Commission of Trinidad and Tobago.

the opposition parties made attempts to form coalitions, the PNM remained, for the most part, in its original form as a single party within the existing political system.

From 1976 to 2010, national politics had been dominated by two political leaders: Basdeo Panday and Patrick Manning, leaders of the UNC and PNM respectively. Panday headed the United Labour Front/UNC most of the time from 1976 to 2010 as opposition leader, except for the period from 1995 to 2002 when he was elected prime minister.

Manning led the PNM from 1986 to 2010, during which time he was also prime minister for two and a half terms (thirteen years). In this context, elections had become a contest between these two political leaders, and the challenge from the opposition perspective had always been how to remove the PNM – the party that had been most in government since independence in 1962. From the PNM's point of view, it was always one of justifying staying in power indefinitely.

The 2010 election was a historic time for the country: for the first time, a woman, Kamla Persad-Bissessar, had unseated both political leaders of the UNC and PNM to become the first woman to lead a coalition movement into government and to change the political landscape of the country.

Overview of the 2000, 2001, 2002, 2007 and 2010 Elections

In 2000, the UNC won the national election with 307,791 (51.7 per cent) votes, gaining nineteen of the thirty-six seats. It was only the second time in the history of Trinidad and Tobago that a political party other than the PNM had won the national election on its own. In 1995, the PNM was replaced in office only because the UNC and the NAR were able to form a coalition. This was historic, as the PNM had governed the country continuously for thirty years, from 1956 to 1986, and for thirty-four years up to the year 2000 – since party government came to Trinidad and Tobago. The PNM had dominated the post-independence period by far.

The day of 11 December 2000 was a historic moment in Trinidad and Tobago. It was the third time that the ruling party, the PNM, was beaten at the election and the first time that the UNC would receive a mandate from the electorate for a second consecutive term. On 10 October 2001, less than one year into the UNC's term in office, a fresh election was called because of internal party bickering. Three party members (namely, Ramesh Lawrence Maharaj, Trevor Sudama and Ralph Maraj) accused the UNC leader of not addressing allegations of corruption in the party. The trio was expelled from the UNC and formed a new political party called Team Unity. The election resulted in a tie, with both PNM and UNC securing eighteen seats each. The decision of President A.N.R. Robinson to ask the opposition PNM to form the government did not sit well with the incumbent UNC and its supporters, and in 2002, unable to govern in a hung parliament, Prime Minister Manning called an early general election on 28 August. This election yielded a PNM victory of twenty seats with 50.89 per cent of the votes. By 2007, when an election was called again, as constitutionally due, the PNM was able to retain power, with a significant victory of twenty-six seats. The UNC had lost considerably, gaining only 29.85 per cent of the votes. Much of the loss in voter support seemed to have come from a split in the UNC, with the emergence of the Congress of the People (COP), which gained 22.71 per cent of the votes in the national election that year (2007), even though it did not win any seats in parliament. A dispute between the UNC's founding leader, Basdeo Panday, and Winston Dookeran, who was the political leader of the UNC, over the role of the leader of the opposition in parliament, resulted in Dookeran being expelled from the UNC and his formation of the COP.

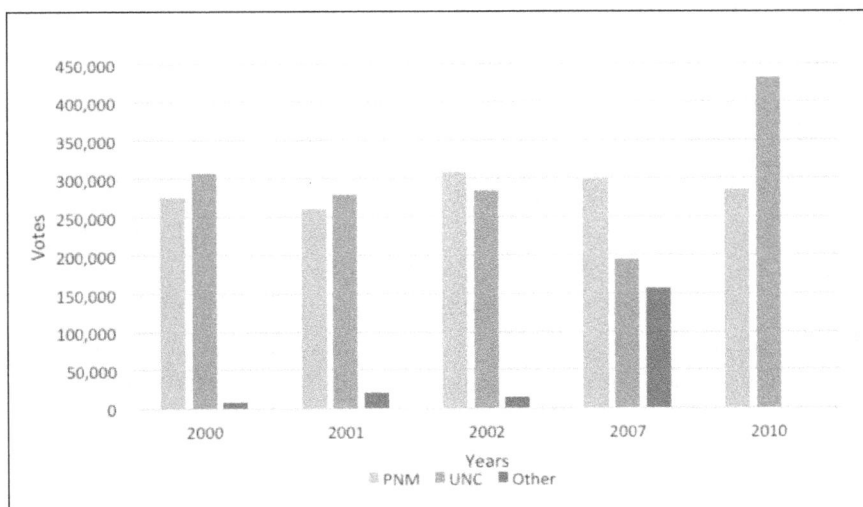

Figure 1. Electoral Outcomes from 2000 to 2010

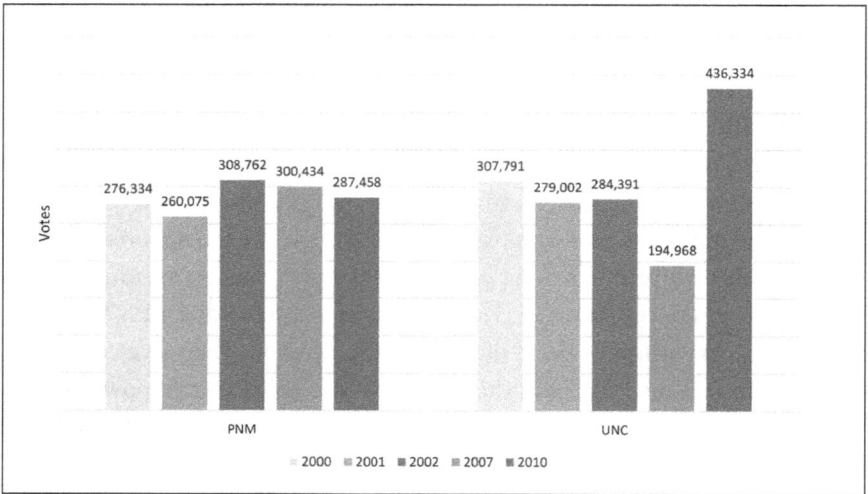

Figure 2. Votes cast for PNM and UNC from 2000 to 2010

Less than two years and five months into his term of government, however, Prime Minister Manning called a fresh election, held on 24 May 2010. This proved to be unfortunate for the Manning-led government, as it resulted in a united force of opposition parties and civic groups, consisting of the UNC, COP, National Joint Action Committee, Movement for Social Justice and Tobago Organisation of the People (TOP), forming a coalition, under the leadership of Kamla Persad-Bissessar, to fight the election. The coalition, known as the PP, won twenty-nine of the forty-one seats to form the 2010 government (a constitutional majority), with the PNM forming the opposition, with twelve seats.

The PP gained 436,334 votes, or 59.8 per cent of the votes, with the PNM gaining only 287,458, or 39.7 per cent, of the votes. The highest voter turnout over the course of a ten-year period in the history of Trinidad and Tobago elections (724,110 votes) was recorded in 2010. The PNM, although losing the election, was still able to maintain its core constituency base, losing by 12,976 votes less than it achieved in the previous election. It appeared that the PP coalition was not able to attract a substantial number of PNM voters but, rather, gained support from new or undecided voters.

Table 2. Trinidad and Tobago Election Results, 2000–2010

Date of Elections	Date Called	Parties Contesting Election	Won	Seats Won	Votes	% of Votes	Total Voter Turnout
11 December 2000	2 November 2000	UNC	UNC	19	307,791	51.70	594,875
		PNM		16	276,334	46.40	
		NAR		1	7,409	1.20	
		Independents		0	1,128	0.19	
		PEP		0	2,071	0.30	
		The Mercy Society		0	142		
10 December 2001	10 October 2001	UNC	Tie (PNM)	18	279,002	49.90	539,175
		PNM		18	260,075	46.31	
		TEAM UNITY		0	14,207	2.30	
		NAR		0	5,841	1.04	
7 October 2005	28 August 2002	PNM	PNM	20	308,762	50.89	606,767
		UNC		16	284,391	46.87	
		NAR		0	6,776	1.12	
		Citizens' Alliance		0	5,983	0.99	
		Democratic Party of T&T		0	662	0.11	
5 November 2007	28 September 2007	PNM	PNM	26	300,434	45.99	653,228
		UNC		15	194,968	29.85	
		COP		0	148,345	22.71	
		DAC		0	8,879	1.36	
		DNA		0	378	0.06	
		Independents		0	241	0.04	
24 May 2010	16 April 2010	People's Partnership:	Coalition	29	436,334	59.80	724,110
		UNC		21	316,600	43.73	
		COP		6	102,265	14.00	
		NJAC/MSJ		0	2,098		
		TOP		2	15,371	2.00	
		PNM		12	287,458	39.70	

Models of Media and Politics

The issue of media and politics in any country must take into account the model of media and politics as an operating framework. The framework may help determine how the media function, but media practice may well determine how the operating model evolves. One of the earliest writings on this subject was *Four Theories of the Press* (1956) by Siebert et al., who developed four models based on their research on three of the most influential nations during that era: the United States, Britain and the Soviet Union. These models are the authoritarian, libertarian, communist and social-responsibility models. Under the authoritarian model, the state was considered the highest institutionalized structure in the land and superseded the individual. The mass media were generally educators and propagandists of the state, even though the media were privately owned. The libertarian theory dated back to the seventeenth century and stressed individual liberties in a climate of free expression. The communist theory arose out of communism, with the sole aim of propagating and expanding the socialist system. Under this model, the media were instruments of governments and integral parts of the state. The social-responsibility model placed more emphasis on press responsibility to society than on press freedom.

These models, although comprehensive, gave a broad outlook on media and politics models in large, developed countries and gave an insight into the type of model that existed in colonial societies under authoritarian regimes, and that continued to exist even after independence in 1962. For instance, under a more authoritarian system during the early independence years, although not a perfect fit for Trinidad and Tobago in any period, the state monopolized public information by limiting licences issued to private individuals to own radio and television stations. During this period and within that context, the media generally acted as the public-relations arm of the state to disseminate information to the wider population, even though a small number of private newspapers existed at that time.

Hallin and Mancini (2004) built on these existing models and developed three more contemporary models: the Mediterranean or polarized-pluralist model, the democratic-corporatist model, and the liberal model. The polarized-pluralist model has an elite-oriented press with relatively small circulation in a state that has a strong role in society. Under this system, journalism was strongly aligned to political activism. Under the democratic-corporatist model, the media were seen as social institutions for which the state had responsibility. Press freedom coexisted with relatively strong state support for and regulation of media. However, under the liberal model, there was early development of press freedom and mass circulation of newspapers in which commercial newspapers dominated and professionalization of journalism was relatively strong, and the parallelism between politicians and journalists was not very strong.

These models focused on large developed countries in North America and western Europe, all of which shared some similarities in history and culture and the evolution of democratic traditions. However, Hallin and Mancini have recognized the limitations of their research in explaining countries with less-developed traditions of media research. Further, they have also acknowledged that these models they have proposed will only apply with considerable adaptation to most other areas in the world.

The sets of models proposed by Siebert et al. and by Hallin and Mancini did not take into account developing countries, especially small island states, as found in the Caribbean. However, on closer examination, the model of media and politics emerging out of Trinidad and Tobago from a tradition of authoritarian regimes in the colonial era has evolved somewhat into a less authoritarian model while moving more towards liberalism in the post-independence era, and especially in the post-1986 period, when deregulation took place under the NAR regime. This model is somewhat similar to the liberal model, which exists in developed countries such as Britain, the United States and Spain, in which the media have considerable freedom and rights under large media systems. The transition period from colonialism to full independence, the developing status of the country and the strong parallelism between media and politics within a small society have been considered in the development of what might constitute an ideal model of media and politics in small island states such as Trinidad and Tobago. Hallin and Mancini's liberal model is important to this study of media and politics in Trinidad and Tobago because of the evolution of the media from state control to an open system with multiple interests. The political system based on parliamentary democracy and a liberal constitution is also relevant, as are the growing independence of the media and the absence of direct state control of privately owned media.

In devising a model for Trinidad and Tobago, a number of models have been studied. Caribbean scholars Rhodes and Henry (1995) studied the media in relation to the state in Antigua and Barbuda, devising a "political resource model" in which the media were viewed as political resources of the state with an identity similar to political parties'. However, they described this model as existing within a repressive political system in which the state owned most of the media and the free press was highly restricted by legislation in that country. They also argued that similar media and politics models existed in the islands of St Kitts, Antigua, Montserrat and Anguilla. This gives an overall picture of media and politics in parts of the region that contrasts with the considerable freedom of the press in Trinidad and Tobago. It is worth mentioning, however, that the Caribbean societies covered by Rhodes and Henry are very small islands, with small populations, in which the state is relatively dominant and government presence is, in general, pervasive.

Wong, in his paper on Asian-based development journalism, examined the 1999 Malaysian election within a framework of an authoritarian, state-dominated model (2004). In a similar study on Malaysia, Abbott (2011) described this model as "electoral authoritarianism", in which the state used legislative checks to "shackle" or control the media. Both Wong and Abbott found that the media demonstrated strong partisan bias to the ruling party, the National Front. Their analysis and findings must be seen in the context of Malaysian media and politics, in which developmental journalism is the working model. The question that arises is whether the notion of free and fair reporting can ever exist in the context of developmental journalism within an authoritarian, state-dominated model of government that dictates the terms of journalistic practice. Although there might be similarities between Malaysia and Trinidad and Tobago, in terms of the diversity of population, the existence of coalition governments and press freedom being enshrined in the constitutions of the respective countries, the model of media and politics is very different in each of these countries.

Journalists in Trinidad and Tobago enjoy tremendous freedom to practise their profession, especially in the post-1986 period, and legislation against media practitioners is only enforced in extreme cases and is generally handled with sensitivity. In June 2012, for instance, the prime minister of Trinidad and Tobago gave a clear commitment to repealing existing defamation leglislation journalists felt constituted inhibition of journalistic freedom. The repeal of a section of the Libel and Defamation Act on criminal libel was passed in parliament in January 2014. Similar action was taken by the Jamaican government in February 2012, when the prime minister established a parliamentary Joint Select Committee to discuss proposals to reform defamation laws. In Malaysia, the situation is complicated by government's ownership or influence, as well as control of the media through party dominance and state power. In Trinidad and Tobago, most of the media is owned by the private sector, and there are strong lines of demarcation between the privately owned and state-owned media. In these models, freedom of the press is directly related to private ownership and independence from direct government influences, although under the liberal system, governments have been known to exert pressure on the free press through other means, such as legislation, withholding of advertising revenues and forcing self-censorship by editors in press establishments.

In their study of the 2006 Singapore election, Cenite et al. (2008) conducted their research on the most popular broadsheet in Singapore: the *Straits Times*. The study highlighted an instance in which the media and the state entered into an accommodation whereby the media were viewed as developmental and supportive of government's policies. Although this system may be beneficial to the state, in contrast, it calls into question the role of the media in the democratic process because in democratic societies, it is assumed that the media will act as a watchdog over matters of national interest if and when required. Under this system, in times of elections, when the state has a tight hold over the media and the media are of the opinion that their role is to be the public-relations arm of government, an opposing party would hardly be given equal amounts of coverage during the campaign period. In such instances, it is expected that the media will exhibit strong structural and partisan bias in favour of the state party during elections. The issue of governance model, media and politics model, role of the press and their effect on democracy are strongly aligned and interconnected and worthy of serious investigation and study.

Gianpietro Mazzoleni's "With the Media, Without the Media: Reasons and Implications of the Electoral Success of Silvio Berlusconi in 2001" (2004) presented a model of media and politics that seems to be unique to Italy and that is a model that can hardly be replicated or exported to other countries. It is assumed that, given the uniqueness of this particular case, in which most of the media were owned or concentrated in the hands of the main candidate at that time, Silvio Berlusconi, there was strong partisan and structural bias in the coverage of the 2001 Italian election campaign. Mazzoleni made a strong case for the mediatization of political campaigns. He surmised, "It is legitimate to assume that if a mogul of this kind enters politics, he has a big advantage over his adversaries, in terms of financial and strategic resources to be employed in marketing his ideas" (Mazzoleni 2004, 269). This strengthens the case for a close examination of ownership and control of media and the implications for bias in coverage and ultimately election outcome. Elements of this model exist in the social-responsibility model found in some Asian countries and some of the small islands in the Caribbean in which the state has a majority-shareholding ownership in the media in their respective countries. Therefore, one might conclude that for democracies truly to evolve, the free media must be allowed to perform their responsibilities as both information brokers and watchdogs of democracy.

Conclusion

Within the context of Trinidad and Tobago and the wider Caribbean, a new model has evolved that is more reflective of the historical background, geographical positioning and cultural nuances of small societies and systems such as exist in the Caribbean. Best described as an emerging liberal-democratic model, this model takes into account the transitioning state of development and governance of the country dominated historically by colonial regimes and authoritarian leadership up to the 1986 period, when the coalition NAR government was elected and deregulation of the media occurred, resulting in a more open system in which the free press has proliferated. It also takes into account the existing small media system, which is highly dependent on state advertising for its survival, as well as the geographic location of the country in terms of proximity and influence of the United States. In addition, the culture of the people and the use of familial and business networks that permeate the entire country have implications in terms of how the media operate and their ability to be objective and balanced. This model also acknowledges that there might be a strong developmental aspect to the media, which have demonstrated considerable commitment and responsibility to upholding the principles of democracy by holding those in power accountable as the country moves towards developed status.

CHAPTER 2

Framing and Bias in Political Campaigns

ELECTION CAMPAIGNS HAVE BEEN ONE OF THE MOST studied forms of communication, especially from the period 1940 onward, as they are short and highly focused events in which the media are intensively used by campaign teams. Trent and Friedenberg (2008, 148) state that during this period, the media are important because they draw attention to candidates while "having tremendous power in determining which news events, which candidates, and which issues are to be covered in any given day". Further, the media are extremely important during campaigns because they frame particular events with a view to "promoting news that will stimulate public support, dampen opposition, and promote the perception that public opinion is in their corner" (Entman 2004, 126). This means that the media have the power to set the political agenda by reporting on certain issues and events while ignoring others. In addition, the mass media force attention to certain issues while constantly presenting objects to suggest what individuals should think about, know about and have feelings about (Lang and Lang 1981). The press "may not be successful much of the time in telling its readers what to think, but it is stunningly successful in telling its readers what to think about" (Cohen 1983, 13). McCombs and Shaw (1972) indicate that the media may have little influence on the direction or intensity of attitudes, but they set the agenda for each political campaign, influencing the salience of attitudes towards the political users.

Although huge sums are spent on media campaigns, it is difficult to find clear evidence that the media decisively influence the outcome of elections. However, during this period, "there is often a more or less institutionalized collusive relationship between politicians or officials and press which may serve a range of purposes without necessarily being manipulative in its effect"

(McQuail 2008, 325). Further, even though political campaigns do not necessarily change the opinion of the voting public, they can easily influence them. However, scholars such as Scheufele (1999) have conceded that media effects on election outcomes have become stronger as the media exert considerable power over the minds of the voting public by framing events in a particular way.

Political campaigns are very important in a country's democratic process, as they determine which party wins an election, and the way a political campaign is conducted is vital in close races (Kenski and Kenski 2005). This is especially true of a country such as Trinidad and Tobago, in which the two major parties represent the two largest ethnic groups of the country, each representing an almost equal percentage of the population. Election results are generally very close and have resulted in deadlock on several occasions.

In Trinidad and Tobago, as in other democracies worldwide, political campaigns are highly mediatized events (Bennett and Entman 2001) in which professional campaigners and communications experts are hired to manage the flow of information; this usually means framing events and setting particular agendas to campaign for the "hearts and minds" of the voting public in the free and paid media (Brader 2006). According to Brader (ibid., 19), "the downside of free media for politicians is that they cannot control the press". Tension occurs when media practitioners refuse to be manipulated by the machinations of politicians and professional campaign/communications managers, insisting on maintaining their independence, integrity and professionalism in conducting their duties. This usually leads to politicians accusing the media of not being objective or being biased against them when they are not featured prominently and positively in the media, especially if they perceive that the media are giving equal or more coverage to the opposition in the run-up to elections. This is especially true of the period 2000–2010, when relations between the media and certain politicians had deteriorated tremendously because of allegations of media bias during campaigning.

Framing Political Campaigns

Framing is defined as "selecting and highlighting some facets of events and issues, and making connections among them so as to promote a particular interpretation, evaluation, and/or solution" (Entman 2004, 5). Entman (1991) noted in his study of the US news treatment of two plane crashes that the manner in which global events were covered and presented to audiences could influence the emergence of a dominant perception. However, McQuail (2008, 378) cited Goffman (1994) "as the originator of the idea that a frame is needed to organize otherwise fragmentary items of experience and information". In the 2008 US election, Entman further noted that framing effects could lead to news slant and bias, and ultimately to political power. He stated that because power is the ability to get others to act as one wants, exerting power to affect behaviour in a democracy requires framing, or telling people what to think about, to influence attitudes that shape their behaviour. Entman further stated that "what matters to successful exertion of political power is whether a frame has a decisive impact on two key audiences – undecided or swing voters and political elites" (2010, 392). This is in keeping with Scheufele's (1999) exposition that framing effects must be posited in the wider media-effects theory of "social constructivism", in which the mass media have a strong effect by constructing or framing social reality in a predictable and patterned way. He also interpreted framing as working to shape and alter audience members' interpretations and preferences through a process which Entman (2010) referred to as priming.

There is little agreement on how to identify frames. Cappella and Jamieson (1997, 47) suggest four criteria: they must have identifiable and linguistic characteristics, must be commonly observed in journalistic practice, must be easily distinguishable from other frames, and must be easily recognized or have representational validity. Frames can range from game frame to horse-race frame, political-strategy frame, news-management frame, politicians-as-individuals frame, conflict frame, governing frame, and episodic frames (Strömbäck and Shehata 2007, 806).

De Vreese (2005) generalized framing by grouping frames as issue-specific or generic. Issue-specific frames, de Vreese says, are pertinent to specific topics or events, whereas generic frames transcend thematic limitations and can be identified in relation to different topics, even over time and cultural contexts. Patterson (1993) explored framing in the context of leadership challenges and strategy; the latter in many ways embracing politics as a horse race and a strategic game. This frame is mostly concerned with the manoeuvring of the candidates and the likely outcome of elections. The overuse of this frame by journalists during elections has been blamed for a "spiral of cynicism" (Cappella and Jamieson 1997) that seduces candidates into concentrating their efforts on playing the game, traps reporters into focusing even more narrowly on that game, and alienates the public from politics. Some of the more common frames used in journalistic research include conflict frames and these have become important in terms of their news value.

Dominant Frames in Trinidad and Tobago Elections

This book refers to a typology of five specific frames – personality, issue, conflict, horse race and governing – as these are easily discernible in the text of published information on elections in the press, while being more relevant within the Caribbean context. Personality frame was chosen because elections in Trinidad and Tobago during the period under study were highly focused on politicians, especially political leaders of the dominant parties: the UNC, the PNM and the PP. In addition, issue-specific framing is very important, as it is important to examine how issues are discussed and how they affect the quality of conversation during campaigns, and ultimately governance of the country after the election. The way issues are framed is a reflection of the role of the media in politics: it follows, then, if issues are not intensely focused on, then the media are more interested in who is contesting the elections and the outcome of elections than the issues.

The use of the horse-race frame has become very prevalent, given the rapid turnover of elections in Trinidad and Tobago during the period from 2000 to 2010, at a rate of one election every two years. The fight has always been between two parties, representing two major ethnic groups, with the challenge being how to unseat the ruling PNM, which held the seat of government since independence on the one hand, and how to keep the opposition at bay on the other. The conflict frame was chosen because conflicts between political parties and among political leaders occur regularly during elections and it has its own cultural resonance, in terms of attracting crowds during political campaigns and selling newspapers; it is also inevitable that once elections are focused on politicians, conflicts will take centre stage on political platforms. The way in which the media portray personal conflicts between politicians or between themselves and politicians is reflective of the maturity of the media in Trinidad and Tobago and has implications for the growth and development of media and politics. The governing frame, as defined in this book, was chosen because of the numerous attempts at unity and coalitions during various periods in the country's political history, which are themes used extensively during political campaigns, especially in 2010, when a coalition of parties emerged victorious at the polls. How this is treated by the media is reflective of the seriousness of those issues during elections. In addition, the issue of good and effective governance in a small, multiethnic, multireligious, ex-colonial island state remains a persistent issue.

Media Bias in Coverage of Political Campaigns

Media bias is important, as most politicians and political parties are of the view that the amount of coverage they receive during elections can have an effect on the outcome of the election, even though McQuail insists that media effects are difficult to prove (McQuail 2005). Politicians have often accused the press of media bias – of framing news in a manner that is uncomplimentary to them and their government or party. On the one hand, politicians try to control the flow of information to the press to ensure that what is reported is in keeping with their agenda and in favour of their policies and positions on issues. On the other hand, the press feels that its main role is to be the "watchdog of democracy" by independently scrutinizing government's activities with the aim of documenting, questioning and investigating those activities. These differing roles have resulted in conflict and tension between politicians and media practitioners, with both groups being suspicious of each other's motives.

Bias is defined as "a pattern of . . . favouritism that occurs when one candidate or party receives more news coverage and more favourable coverage over an extended period of time" (Kenney and Simpson 2003, cited in Cenite et al. 2008, 284). Researchers have identified a range of biases found in electoral coverage, such as framing bias (Entman 2010), structural bias, partisan bias (Strömbäck and Shehata 2007), reputational bias (Hayes 2008), gatekeeping bias, coverage bias, statement bias (Barber 2008), and cultural bias (Garyantes 2006). The way the media prime a particular point of view or stress the salience of particular issues could convey a sense of bias towards a particular political party. These biases in turn could be informed by their own cultural and partisan views, as well as the structural orientation of their media houses, referred to by Entman as schemas stored in their brain as prior knowledge.

Balance is defined as "aiming for neutrality and requires that reporters present the views of legitimate spokespersons of the conflicting sides in any significant dispute, and provide both sides with roughly equal attention"

(Entman 1989, cited in Cenite et al. 2008, 284). "Objective", in contrast, means the "reporting of something called 'news' without commenting on it, slanting it, or shaping its formulation in any way" (Schudson 2001, cited in Garyantes 2006, 3). Schudson further states that objectivity "guides journalists to separate facts from values and to report only the facts" (Garyantes 2006, 3). Other theorists define objectivity as "the collection and dissemination of information that describes reality as accurately as possible" (Ryan 2001, 3).

The general conclusion, therefore, is that media bias was very much a part of election coverage around the world, and the key issue that emerged was not whether media bias existed, but that there were variations within the realm of bias as a result of a variety of circumstances that influenced journalistic practices.

Researching Bias and Framing in National Elections

My research has drawn from Westerstahl's (1983) concept of balance, which involves the amount of negative and positive coverage given to political parties during elections. However, Westerstahl (1983, 419) does suggest that some deviations from strict balance can be expected and tolerated if one party remains silent or events "pertain to one party only" and the "character of the event may be such that the party is placed in a more positive or negative light". To obtain more conclusive evidence on the correlation between framing and bias, during the 2000–2010 period under study, a bias scale (figure 3) was developed using clearly defined codes to unravel the five frames being examined in the newspapers. These codes were applied to clippings from front pages and news stories from 582 editions of the three dailies, *Guardian*, *Express* and *Newsday*, during the five campaign periods. The frames were then scaled (table 3) to determine whether they were negative, positive or balanced towards government or the opposition party.

If the news item was more focused on the issue of the day and presented objectively the views of contending parties, then it was taken that this was a balanced article, as it did not focus on the political parties or the personalities of either side (see table 3). This scaling was administered to all front pages and political news stories during the five campaign periods. To some extent, the scaling relied on the objectivity of the researcher in applying elements of the scale evenhandedly and classifying the articles appropriately.

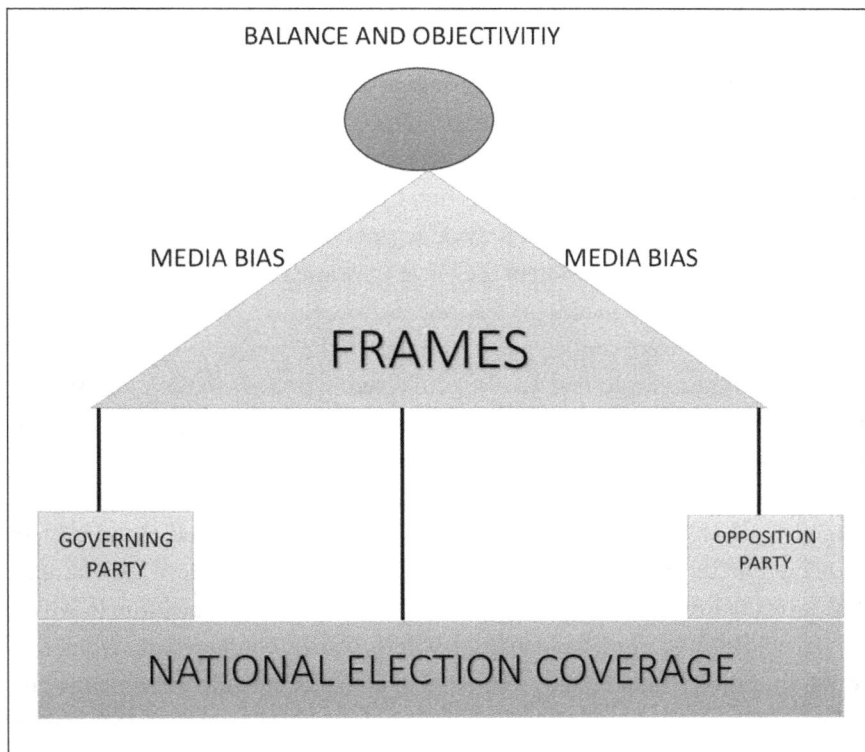

Figure 3. Bias scale

Table 3. Sample Scale

Headline	Positive (+)	Negative (−)	Balance (B)	Positive (+)	Negative (−)	Balanced (B)
Photo	+	−	B	+	−	B
Issue	+	−	B	+	−	B

In addition, all editorials and a sampling of the political commentaries were examined to determine the major themes emanating from these writings; these writings were compared over the five elections with the views expressed in interviews with senior journalists in all three newspapers to come to conclusions about the positions taken by editors, media owners and opinion leaders. Bias can manifest itself in a number of ways, as discussed here.

Cultural Bias

Dianne Garyantes, in her paper, "Coverage of the Iraqi Elections: A Textual Analysis of Al-Jazeera and the *New York Times*" (2006), on the coverage of the 2005 Iraqi election, stated that framing has been associated with potential bias when the coverage involved other cultures. She emphasized one type of bias – cultural bias – which she found prevalent among journalists in Iraq. Cultural bias was found in the omission of the views of women when reporting on news in Iraq and within the media profession, as that country was an Islamist state, in which women were traditionally relegated to the background as support to their spouses and rarely, if at all, were involved in politics in their country. In Trinidad and Tobago, even though the country has strong religious traditions such as Catholicism, Protestantism, Evangelicalism, Hinduism and Islam, and communities of various sects, religion is not a dominant force in election campaigns. And although women have been traditionally viewed as support to their men in Trinidad and Tobago, the role of women in society has changed dramatically over the decades because of the influence of education, in which the participation of women outstrips that of their male counterparts. Women in contemporary Trinidad have progressed in all fields, including the media and politics. In fact, 2010 could be considered a milestone for women in these fields, as a woman became the first female prime minister of the country; in turn, all three dailies were headed by female editors-in-chief in 2012: Therese Mills of *Newsday,* Omatie Lyder of the *Express* and Judy Raymond of the *Guardian.* However, even though women have made considerable progress, they are still subjected to some level of cultural bias, as Trinidad and Tobago has historically been a patriarchal society in which women, especially Hindu women, were ascribed traditional roles in the home.

Partisan Reputational Bias

In "Party Reputations, Journalistic Expectations: How Issue Ownership Influences Election News" (2008), author Danny Hayes linked media bias to media favourability on issue ownership in his study of three US presidential elections: 1992, 1996 and 2000. Hayes stated that the underlying assumption of favourability was that if news was slanted in a way that benefited one candidate or party over the other, public opinion could be affected. Hayes did acknowledge that the editorial position of a newspaper affected the favourability of coverage, and that this was linked to the business side of journalism and the political orientation of the newspaper (Druckman and Parkin 2005; Kahn and Kenney 2002). He further stated that a candidate's standing in the poll could affect coverage and that popular candidates might receive more favourable treatment from journalists. He argued that in terms of issue ownership (Petrocik 1996), a party's reputational advantages in different policy domains influenced the favourability of news coverage towards candidates during campaigns (Hayes 2008), resulting in a subtle type of bias or partisan reputational bias.

Airtime and Line-up Bias/Gatekeeping Bias

Marsha Barber (2008) examined media bias from the perspective of airtime and line-up bias in three major Canadian networks: ABC, CBS and NBC. She defined airtime bias as the allocation of airtime to each party and its leaders. She elaborated that her study, by extension, focused on gatekeeping and coverage bias. Gatekeeping bias she defined as the preference for selecting stories from one party rather than another. Her underlying assumption was that media coverage did have the potential to influence the outcome of an election. She focused on measuring the volume of coverage and the news line-up, which she argued was grounded in gatekeeping theory. In addition, Barber demonstrated how bias manifested itself in other media outside of print and presented a broad view of media bias in general.

Coverage Bias/Agenda Bias/Statement Bias

In exploring the 2006 Dutch election (Takens et al. 2008, 1–27) "coverage bias" was defined as "the extent to which the amount of news coverage devoted to political parties is incommensurate with the strength of their political base". Agenda bias, they stated, deals with "the extent to which the media attention for [sic] different issues reflects the diversity of the issues in social reality" (ibid., 3). They described "statement bias" as focusing "on the actual content of coverage, namely the tone of the news, or the degree to which positive and/or negative statements about the political parties and their politicians are made" (ibid., 3). Takens et al. made a strong case for how the media were able to set the agenda by their choice of what constituted news, especially in their coverage of political news; further, if particular parties were to own certain issues, then it could be assumed that a party owning a particular issue would receive more media coverage during elections when that particular issue was dominant. In such a situation, Takens et al. argued that the media would be guilty of bias, as by choosing to highlight the issues raised by that party while downplaying the views of an opposing party on that issue, they inevitably created a context of bias.

Structural and Partisan Bias

In a study of Britain and Sweden, Strömbäck and Shehata (2007) added a new dimension to bias by linking structural bias to agenda-setting theory. In "Structural Biases in British and Swedish Election News Coverage", they defined structural bias as norms of journalism or reporter behaviour which favoured news about some topics over others and argued that this news emphasis advantaged some candidates and disadvantaged others. They also indicated that structural bias was identified with episodic framing (Iyengar 1991); tended to be event-centred, detached, and focused on bad news as well as on politics as strategy, and tactics rather than policies; and was highly dependent on official viewpoints (Schudson 2003). The authors also conceptualized structural bias as involving a linkage between the system-level functions and media content. They explained: "If structural bias is rooted in journalistic norms as well as in the processes and circumstances of news productions, and these are different in countries belonging to different models of media and politics; it follows that the news coverage of elections should display different characteristics in these countries" (Strömbäck and Shehata 2007, 800). In Trinidad and Tobago, evidence points to structural bias in sourcing information from official viewpoints while focusing on bad news.

Zeldes et al. (2008) focused on media bias and its two attributes: structural and partisan bias. They alluded to media bias as an abstract idea linked to ethics and credibility; however, they maintained that no professional consensus existed on what were the ethical norms that applied, and further, that there were no standards in place to ensure that these qualities were met. They sought to explain the imbalance in the 2004 US presidential election by looking at both structural and partisan bias. They defined structural bias as having to do with journalistic values, resources and outside influences in processing and reporting news, and partisan bias with journalists' political orientations in favour of one candidate over the other.

Allegations of Media Bias during Elections in Trinidad and Tobago

Allegations of media bias have been levelled against the local media by politicians, especially the prime ministers of the country, beginning with this country's first premier and prime minister, Eric Williams, as far back as the late 1950s, in the pre-independence era. Williams was of the opinion that the established press, the *Trinidad Guardian*, was biased against him and his brand of politics and was favourable to the colonial status quo. At that time, the PNM was viewed as a revolutionary party representing the black working class in a society in which power was held by the wealthy business sector, comprising mainly affluent white men. The *Trinidad Guardian* was owned by wealthy private individuals who represented the status quo. Similarly, all political leaders of the country thereafter had their conflicts with the press and, at certain points during their careers, accused it of bias on various occasions.

Prime Minister Eric E. Williams

In April 1960, Eric Williams, first prime minister of the country, marched in the rain, together with thousands of nationals, to Woodford Square and ritualistically burned documents described as "the seven deadly sins" (Ryan 2009, 196), one of which was the *Trinidad Guardian*. According to political scientist Selwyn Ryan, the *Guardian* and Williams were virtually at war from 1955 onward. Ryan claimed that before the arrival of Williams on the political scene, the *Guardian* was "the major influence moulding public opinion". Ryan traced this open war between the established press at that time and the first prime minister to the *Guardian*'s bias towards Albert Gomes, a local politician of Portuguese ancestry. Ryan argued that from the perspective of the *Guardian*, Gomes provided the ideal type of leadership needed at that time. On the eve of the 1956 election, the paper attacked Williams as "a dictator" and published a portrait of him next to one of Adolf Hitler. Nevertheless, Ryan stated that the paper did endorse Williams, together with two of his colleagues, on the eve of that election.

Although Williams won the 1956 general election, relations continued to be strained between the prime minister and that newspaper for most of his years of leadership of Trinidad and Tobago. Veteran journalist George John (2002, 183) described the *Guardian* as "a subscriber to the politics of the Chamber of Commerce", stating that the *Guardian* was out of sympathy with Williams and just would not come to terms with his rise to power. John further argued that the newspaper fought a monumental battle on behalf of the conservatives and the more or less upper-business-class elements of society, who were suspicious of Williams's politics. He also said that the newspaper's tactics were often unfair and hinted at a Catholic bias in its writing, as well as a bias towards foreign news, mainly from England. Catholics at that time constituted the largest religious minority in Trinidad and Tobago, which is a multireligious, multiethnic society. During this period, the *Guardian* was owned by an English-based company, Thomson Newspapers, and was staffed mostly by English journalists or middle-class locals who supported the status quo – mainly local whites.

Local media mogul Ken Gordon also recounted an incident with Prime Minister Williams in which he was also branded "anti-PNM" in his early career at the Chamber of Commerce, and later at the *Express* newspaper. He indicated that while attending a press conference in 1974, in his capacity as programme director of Radio Trinidad, he insisted that Williams answer a question that was not placed on the agenda before the press conference. The prime minister accused him of being impertinent and abruptly terminated the press conference. Gordon described the relationship between the *Express* and Williams as one of "ongoing conflict" (Gordon 1999), implying that this had to a large degree been because of that single incident, in which he had got on the wrong side of the prime minister. The fact that Gordon was a member of the Chamber of Commerce might have served to worsen the situation: the Chamber of Commerce comprised the business leadership and the establishment at that time and became one of the prime minister's favourite "whipping boys".

Prime Minister George Chambers

When Williams died in office in 1981, he was succeeded by George Chambers. A general election was held, as scheduled, in 1981. Chambers led the PNM to a twenty-six-seat majority in parliament. Chambers represented an opportunity for renewal of party and government, which had served continuously since

1956, and consequently a possible change in approach to governance. However, during his five-year term as prime minister (1981–1986), relations soured between the prime minister and the press. During the election campaign of 1986, in which there was convergence of a number of parties into a united opposition against the Chambers-led PNM, and against the background of an economic recession triggered by a dramatic fall in oil prices, which cut the country's per capita income by half, Chambers got into a direct confrontation with the media. This proved to be the turning point in the relationship between Prime Minister Chambers and the press. On 23 November 1986, at the PNM's presentation of candidates in Arima, the prime minister refused to speak until state-owned Trinidad and Tobago Television (TTT) removed its lights and microphone, resulting in reporters from both the print and electronic media being verbally and physically threatened by supporters of the PNM party. TTT, led by Jones P. Madeira, was forced to leave the political meeting.

Express political reporter Ria Taitt, who covered the 1986 presentation of candidates by Chambers, reported that she was "pelted with ice, red-mango seeds, tamarind seeds and paper cups" (Taitt 1986, 3). Prime Minister Chambers stated that he was reacting to what he perceived as biased reporting of his stewardship during the 1986 political campaign. Francis Prevatt, chairman of the PNM, wrote to TTT chairman Frank Barsotti complaining that the PNM had "publicly drawn attention and objected on more than one occasion to the bias against the PNM your organisation has been showing" (Johnson 1986, 1). On 19 November 1986, the *Daily Express* also reported on its front page: "Static Follows the PM's Attack on 610", stating that employees of state-owned National Broadcasting Service Radio had asked management to issue a public statement in response to statements made by the prime minister that the station was biased against the PNM in the 1986 election, and that the station was "one of four arms of the local media which were opposing the People's National Movement in the coming election." On 25 November 1986, the *Express*, on its front page, published an article titled "Absolutely No Excuse for Mr Chambers' Behaviour", condemning the prime minister's attack against both the state-owned media and the *Express* and stating it was "tantamount to a declaration of war against the media". The newspaper further stated that it was a "direct threat to independence of thought and action in society". Two days later, on 27 November, the *Express* published a half-apology by Chambers on its front page in which he stated that "nobody had defended the press in Trinidad and

Tobago as he had" and that he was upset over the disrespect shown to his office and the people of the country, rather than to him personally.

Prime Minister Basdeo Panday

In 1996, Basdeo Panday, UNC political leader and prime minister of the country, became antagonistic towards the media and directed his cabinet not to speak to the *Guardian* because he thought that its editor-in-chief, Jones P. Madeira, was "racist and spiteful". Panday was responding to a front-page *Guardian* headline entitled "Chutney Rising", which featured a photo of him with a drink in his hand. Chutney is a spicy version of East Indian music that is associated with heavy alcohol consumption. The coded message implied through the association of the headline; the prime minister, who was of East Indian descent; and the drink in his hand offended Panday. His angry public reaction set off a chain of events that would eventually lead to Madeira resigning from the *Guardian*. It also led to a historic march by journalists and other media personnel for "Democracy, Human Rights and Free Press", which attracted popular support from the opposition parties, trade unions and nationals of the country.

In 1997, open conflict flared between Prime Minister Panday and head of the *Express*, Ken Gordon, over Gordon's condemnation of the contents of the Green Paper "Reform of Media Law: Towards a Free and Responsible Media". Gordon stated that it was an attempt by the UNC-led government to curb media freedom and to regulate the free press. Panday accused Gordon of being a pseudo-racist "to maintain his monopolistic advantage over his competitors in the media" (Gordon 1999, 168). This incident further eroded the relationship between the *Express* and Panday and resulted in a lengthy battle between the two in the courts of Trinidad and Tobago.

In 1998, Panday again declared war on the media during a political rally at Mid-Centre Mall in Chaguanas, calling on supporters to treat the media as "enemies". The rally ended with reporters being assaulted by supporters of the party. In 1999, Panday lost his temper and screamed at TV6 reporter Natalie Williams, "That's insulting!" when asked a provocative question about whether he would unduly favour his friends at Inncogen during a groundbreaking ceremony for the Inncogen power plant (*Sunday Guardian*, 9 November 2008, A8–A9).

Panday again got into conflict with the media in 2001, when he publicly attacked the *Express* for investigating corruption during his tenure of governance. Panday described the newspaper as the "enemy" and told supporters "to train their guns on that house" (*Express*, 14 November 2001). Panday also accused that newspaper of being biased towards the PNM and against his government.

Prime Minister Patrick Manning

PNM political leader and prime minister Patrick Manning too had his fair share of battles with the media in Trinidad and Tobago, in which he felt that the media were being unduly harsh on his government. In 2004, Manning accused state-owned TTT of attempting to present the PNM government as "dictatorial". He called on media houses to act responsibly, as there was a "considerable amount of bias, character assassination and slander which passes for journalism" (*Sunday Guardian*, 9 November 2008, A8–A9).

Relations between Manning and the media reached an all-time low on 25 October 2008, when Manning, in angry response to two radio broadcasters on 94.1 FM on the issue of government's decision to raise the cost of premium gas and the high cost of converting vehicles to compressed-natural-gas use, stormed into the radio station to chastise the two broadcasters, Kevin Baker and David Murray, for their lack of professionalism, which led to the two employees' being suspended. His action resulted in open warfare between the media and the prime minister, with government ministers Colm Imbert and Conrad Enill openly condemning the media's action and accusing them of biased reporting (*Express*, 15 November 2008, A18). It also started a series of articles including editorials, news stories and commentaries on press freedom and the role of the press in a democracy. Both the Trinidad and Tobago Publishers and Broadcasters Association and Media Association of Trinidad and Tobago publicly condemned the prime minister's actions, and it even became a topic of discussion in the parliament of Trinidad and Tobago. This matter seemed to have been resolved behind closed doors, and the issue temporarily disappeared from the public domain in 2008. The suspended broadcasters at the radio station were subsequently reinstated.

However, two years later, the issue of media bias against the PNM and the prime minister arose again during the campaign for the 2010 election. At a PNM political meeting on 21 May, Minister Colm Imbert called on supporters "to deal with the media" over coverage of the 2010 general election, stating "they are not with us", and suggesting the media were conspiring against the PNM (*Guardian*, 21 May 2010, A5). Imbert continued to accuse the media of not being balanced in their reporting during an interview with the *Guardian* (16 March 2010). A similar view was taken by Minister Conrad Enill during an interview conducted by journalist Andy Johnson of the *Express*, in which he reiterated that the media were hostile to the PNM and that most of their achievements were lost to the population because of biased reporting (6 May 2010, 12). Prime Minister Manning also lashed out at the media during a political meeting, alleging a media plot against him and his party (*Guardian*, 28 May 2010, A5). In response to these allegations, Manning was asked to reconsider his position by *Guardian* columnist Tony Fraser (28 April 2010, A28), who reiterated the role of the fourth estate and the professionalism with which journalists conducted their duties.

Perception of Media Bias by Nationals of Trinidad and Tobago

In 2009, a survey conducted by the British firm Market and Opinion Research International (MORI) indicated that the public considered the media generally neutral when reporting about government, but where there was a perception of bias, more people considered them to be pro-government than anti-government (MORI and Associates 2009). The MORI survey was commissioned by the PNM government and was based on 689 in-house interviews with nationals, a representative sample of the population of Trinidad and Tobago. The findings of the MORI survey were in contradiction to the allegations of bias being made by Prime Minister Manning and the PNM party. A similar survey was conducted by the ANSA McAL Psychological Research Centre at the University of the West Indies in May 2010; its findings were similar to those of the MORI survey. More than 64 per cent of respondents stated that they did not think that the media were biased towards any of the political parties. Only 10 per cent said the media were biased towards the PNM, whereas 6 per cent felt that they were biased towards the UNC. Eleven per cent of respondents said they were biased towards both UNC and PNM. The ANSA McAL survey was done on the eve of the 2010 election, when Manning and some members of his cabinet had accused the media of biased reporting during the 2010 campaign. Both surveys, which were separately commissioned during the PNM reign, covering a period of two years and leading up to the 2010 election, demonstrated that although the PNM strongly believed the media were biased against it, the general perception by nationals was that the media were not biased, and in fact, tended to lean more in favour of the ruling PNM party.

There is no known survey of perceptions of bias by the population before 2009; however, a study of ethnicity and the media in Trinidad and Tobago conducted by the Centre for Ethnic Studies at the University of the West Indies in 1995, examining how various ethnic groups perceived the various media regarding the reporting of news and cultural and social events, indicated that a large majority of East Indians (66 per cent) and Africans (63 per cent) thought the *Express* was fair in reporting the news. Similarly, 68 per cent of the Indian population and 67 per cent of the African population also thought the *Guardian* was fair in its reporting of news. Similar trends were found among other ethnic groups (Ryan and McCree 1995). Although the study was in keeping with perceptions of news reporting in 2009 and 2010, it concluded that the media in Trinidad and Tobago did exhibit three forms of bias: creole, urban and class, in favour of the lighter-skinned middle class.

Media's Perception of Biased Reporting of National Elections

In interviews conducted with select media practitioners, all of whom worked in the press and covered elections at various points in their career, they all agreed that even though the media strove for objectivity, media bias could occur in political coverage and be sustained consistently over a long period of time by certain journalists who covered elections, and that they had seen evidence of bias exhibited by their colleagues in the media during national elections. Further, they agreed that bias occurred mainly because of poor supervision by editors who were weak, untrained or themselves the victims of their own personal biases. Other reasons ranged from partisanship on the part of journalists, media managers, or owners of media houses, in terms of their personal preferences for a particular political party; personal problems between journalists and politicians in which certain journalists felt slighted or ill-treated, leading to their taking a particular position; lack of proper training; and lack of journalistic integrity. They also felt that bias occurred when media houses were unable to resist the "scoop", even when it had been acquired under compromised circumstances. Further, that bias was demonstrated by certain columnists because they had the power to make politicians into heroes or victims, depending on how they were framed.

In terms of the 2010 election, it was felt that the media were much too nervous about being seen as taking sides on political issues because of fear of what the political/business realities were, given that newspapers were heavily dependent on state advertising. The media members stated that although there were achievements by the PNM, the non-achievements and absolute bad decision-making by the political leader far overwhelmed the good decisions. The media responded to the bad decisions made by the government during its eight or nine years in office. In addition to the media's taking a position in columns, there was an overwhelming sense from the population that government had gone wrong, and this was reflected in television/print media. The media were reflecting citizens' sense of unease and dissatisfaction with the performance of government.

Further, during consecutive election campaigns, not exclusively in the 2010 campaign, it was felt that an unhealthily close relationship between certain journalists and politicians created fertile conditions for orchestration of the release of information as news stories and for political manipulation of the media. However, those journalists who were aligned to political parties did so in subtle ways, and the evidence was seen after the election, when certain reporters accepted lucrative positions in the state media.

However, the interviewees felt there was clear evidence of gender bias against the opposition leader, Kamla Persad-Bissessar, as the first female prime minister of the country, even though she personified those qualities the country wanted in a prime minister at that time. These qualities were in direct contrast to those the country had started to dislike about the PNM political leader; further, she presented a novelty in terms of the timing with which she won the leadership of the UNC, together with the fact that she was heading a coalition.

When questioned on whether bias occurred outside the 2010 election, the interviewees felt that 1986 was an outstanding example of the print media in particular rallying in active support of a political entity. In the 1986 election, the media definitely sided with the NAR; this was done in context of there having been one party in government for thirty years. Further, so much had occurred over the years in terms of accumulating dirt on the PNM that it was almost inevitable that a new force that seemed to be uniting the country would find favour in 1986. The opinion of the media at that time was that there was a need for change, and this was the first time disparate forces presented themselves striving for coherence. The media wanted change, and the moment had arrived for national unity, as no built-up allegiance, but elements of disparate and disjointed forces began to coalesce.

Conclusion

It is clear that media bias has been an issue during the last fifty years at least for politicians in power, their political parties and sitting prime ministers. It is instructive that polls conducted in 2009 and 2010 indicated that the general population did not agree that there was media bias against the sitting government. Although polls do not exist that measure this factor for other years, there is a likelihood that public opinion on this matter would probably be the same over time. However, interviews conducted with senior media practitioners in the field indicated that bias can in fact occur, and acknowledgement that bias both of a partisan and structural nature can exist, and in fact has occurred, needs to be taken into account. The distinction among reporter bias, editorial bias and commentator bias is important: even if the media strive for balance, certain behaviours, events and issues can tip the scale, and complex factors might conspire to contribute to bias. For the most part, the media tend to reflect the mood of the country, and the evidence suggests that incumbency might be at a disadvantage during an election, as the incumbent is almost inevitably forced to defend a record of performance while the opposition is free to criticize and proffer new ideas, proposals and solutions. The media, of course, report what politicians say, which the citizen reads, forming opinions from day to day. In this context, the conduct of a campaign, the framing of issues by party communications specialists, and the translation of these by the media become important factors in the consolidation of public opinion and in exerting influence on how the citizenry thinks.

CHAPTER 3

The Evolution of Media in Trinidad and Tobago

THE EVOLUTION, GROWTH AND DEVELOPMENT OF THE PRESS and press freedom in Trinidad and Tobago must be seen in the context of the parallel development of the system of media and its implications for media and politics. The period covered is postcolonial, during which first self-government and then independence and republicanism came to Trinidad and Tobago. State ownership of the media was dominant in the period after independence (1962) to 1986, which was also a period of state expansion across the economic sectors. In a sovereign state, both radio and television played a developmental role and generally propagated government's policies through the dissemination of information to the wider public.

Historically, the government of Trinidad and Tobago had a monopoly over broadcast media, with state ownership of the only national television station, TTT, and National Broadcasting Service, the state-owned radio station, respectively. TTT started as a private company on 1 November 1962 before being acquired by the government in 1969 and becoming the state broadcaster for more than thirty years. Before this, electronic media were mainly radio, with full-time broadcasting starting in 1947 with the establishment of Radio Trinidad by Trinidad Broadcasting Limited. This was the main form of communication used by the state to reach the population (Task Force on Telecommunications 1989). In the early days of independence in Trinidad and Tobago, the state media, including the Government Information Division, were used by the government to disseminate information about government policies to the wider population, and it would not be unfair to describe the role of these institutions as public-relations and communications agents of the Trinidad and Tobago government.

The Importance of the Daily Press in Trinidad and Tobago

In a small country such as Trinidad, with a population of just 1.3 million, there are only three daily newspapers: the *Express, Guardian* and *Newsday*, each having a dedicated readership comprising different socio-economic groups. Newspapers are very popular sources of information and are therefore constantly in demand by loyal readers who are mostly interested in local events and issues, although some coverage is dedicated to both regional and international events. Sunday newspapers especially are in high demand by readers who read ritualistically as part of their leisure activities.

In Trinidad, the weekly newspapers include the *Bomb*, the Friday *Mirror* and Sunday *Mirror*, all of which are highly sensational and target very specific readerships. Similarly, Tobago has its own newspaper, *Tobago News*, which focuses mostly on events and issues relating specifically to that island. The three dailies in Trinidad are also distributed to Tobago as well. Therefore, reading newspapers, especially the three dailies, is very much a part of the culture of both Trinidad and Tobago.

During national elections, newspapers are commodities in high demand because they are one of the foremost sources of political information for the population; this was especially true during 2000–2010. Therefore, during political campaigns, the daily newspapers become significantly more important to political parties for both coverage and advertising to reach the widest number of members of the voting public possible. Weeklies do not garner the same interest, as they have a reputation of being anti-establishment and are generally perceived as being negative towards most governing parties.

Newspapers are written by varied authors with different intents and purposes. Front pages and editorials are determined by in-house editors, who choose photos and headlines based on newsworthiness and timeliness, mainly to attract wide readership. In contrast, editorials, which are mostly written in-house, focus on a wide range of topical issues, especially politics, and are more concerned with ensuring that politicians are accountable to the citizenry for policy decisions and issues relating to governance. News stories are written by journalists, who cover daily events – reporting the news as it occurs, with the main objective being to provide information on daily occurrences during an election campaign. Commentaries, in contrast, are written by a variety of people representing the pluralistic views of a wide variety of individuals and groups. A very small number of seasoned journalists also write columns. However, in all three newspapers, editorials, ownership and opinion-leaders' policies tend to be distinct and separate, although there might be some discernible alignment of intent and purpose.

Trinidad Guardian

The oldest and most conservative of the three dailies, the *Trinidad Guardian* started as a broadsheet in 1917 and was owned by a British company, the Thomson Corporation. During the pre-independence and early independence periods, the *Guardian*, which had a reputation for supporting the elite class in society as well as the status quo, developed a reputation for being anti-government because it did not support Eric Williams, who was leading a nationalist movement, during the 1956 election.

By 2012, the *Guardian* was still considered generally supportive of the status quo and had a loyal, older, more conservative readership. This paper was considered generally supportive of business and private-sector interests. The newspaper was converted to a tabloid in 2002, and subsequently to a smaller format in 2008 to compete with its main rival, the *Express*. The *Guardian* was sold to the ANSA McAL Group of Companies, a private conglomerate with diverse business interests involving real estate, finance, car dealerships and manufacturing, to name a few. The company also owns both radio and television stations. The newspaper is currently owned by Guardian Media Limited, the media sector of ANSA McAL, which has its own board of directors. In keeping with international trends, the newspaper is also available online at www. guardian.co.tt. It is the only newspaper that has partnered with the University of the West Indies ANSA McAL Psychological Research Centre to conduct regular polls on elections, which are published in the *Sunday Guardian*. These polls also focus on major issues concerning government representation and serve as a guide to political leaders in terms of their performance, as well as providing feedback to nationals on how select demographics feel about issues relating to politics.

Express

The *Express* emerged out of the collapse of the *Daily Mirror* on 6 June 1967, with Patrick Chookolingo being its first general manager and Owen Baptiste its founding editor. George John, one of its earliest editors, in his memoirs hinted at a strong pro-business slant and anti-PNM bias facilitated by Ken Gordon, who had succeeded Chookolingo as general manager. The *Express* is currently published by the Caribbean Communications Network (CCN), which also owns TV6 and a number of local radio stations. CCN is a subsidiary of One Caribbean Media Limited, which was formed in 2006 as a result of a merger between CCN and the Barbados Nation Corporation. One Caribbean Media operates from Trinidad, Barbados, Grenada, St Lucia and the Eastern Caribbean and owns both print and electronic media. As the most widely read local newspaper, the *Express* goes beyond business readership and reaches the middle class as well as lower-income groups in the society. A survey by local research company Market Facts and Opinion conducted in March 2012 revealed that the *Express* was the number-one choice of readers, with daily readership (Monday–Friday) increasing by 6 per cent from the last survey conducted in 2009, whereas weekend readership, especially that of the *Sunday Express*, had increased by 11 per cent, dominating the market, especially in the age group of fifteen to nineteen years. In 2014, the *Express* dominated the local market, with 49 and 57 per cent readership for weekdays and weekends respectively. The newspaper has a readership of approximately seventy-five thousand, representing 40 per cent of the reading population of the country. Similar to the *Guardian*, the *Express* also publishes political polls, such as those conducted by the North American Caribbean Teachers Association, headed by New York–based pollster Vishnu Bisram. These polls are also published in the other two dailies in Trinidad.

Newsday

The third daily, *Newsday*, is the newest paper on the market and was first headed in 1993 by Therese Mills, a former editor-in-chief of the *Guardian*. The newspaper is published by Daily News Limited and owned by a number of private individuals. The format, design and layout of the newspaper are similar to the tabloid size of the *Express*. However, its content is focused more on news reporting, rather than commentaries by columnists, although there is a small group of invited people who write consistently on varied issues. This paper generally reaches lower-income groups within the ages of thirty-five to fifty-five years; however, it has been steadily growing in popularity over the years. By 2014, *Newsday* had become the second most read newspaper, replacing the *Guardian* and capturing 33 and 30 per cent of the market share for weekdays and weeklies respectively.

Deregulation and Expansion of Media

With the change in government from the PNM to the NAR, a cabinet committee was appointed on 17 June 1987 to develop a national policy on telecommunications in Trinidad and Tobago. The mandate of the committee was to study the use of the airwaves, especially the use of satellites; the granting of radio and television licences; and all sound and visual broadcasting. This committee recommended the creation of a new regulatory body, the Telecommunications Authority, as well as the establishment of an appropriate telecommunications regulatory framework to "promote greater private sector participation in the sector as well as support a multiple network operator and service provider environment". In terms of broadcasting, the group also recommended that government "identify the number of available frequencies and establish a transparent and non-discriminatory procedure for allocation of licences" (Cabinet Minute No. 1481, 1987). Further, licences were not required by authorized network providers for Internet services. The committee recommended for immediate action the introduction of new cellular technology and the award of a second mobile phone operator (Task Force on Telecommunications 1989).

As a result, the monopolistic communications system that had existed from pre-independence through thirty years of one-party rule was opened up, and more licences were granted for private individuals and companies to own radio and television stations. This also created a cellular revolution while allowing a second provider, the Irish-based cellular company Digicel, to enter the market along with local provider Telecommunications Services of Trinidad and Tobago. Cellular phones became the most popular form of communication in the country. An amendment to the Telecommunications Authority Act (Act 40 of 1991) was finally passed in parliament on 28 May 2001.

By 2012, in a population of 1.3 million people, there were twenty television stations, of which eight were free-to-air, one available via cable and nine subscription television broadcasts. There were thirty-eight radio stations, of which only one was AM broadcasting, with the rest being FM stations. There were also eleven newspapers and nine Internet service providers.

In a time of deregulation of the media, the monopolistic media system that existed in Trinidad and Tobago in the colonial era and early independence period transitioned towards a freer system of media, in which the print and electronic media began to fashion themselves along the lines of the BBC in Britain and CNN in the United States. The press took its role as watchdogs of democracy very seriously, striving to be fair and objective in its reporting as the "fourth estate" while maintaining close links with government as a major source of information. Access to CNN only became available in Trinidad and Tobago with the introduction of cable television in 1999; the Internet had become the most popular and accessible source of news information around the world. These facts, together with the opening of the media at home, had an effect on both the media's and journalists' perception of their roles.

State Regulation

The opening up of the monopolistic regulatory system after 1986 resulted in renewed problems of regulating media content from cable, satellite and national television, as well as radio and print media. In 2001, the government, through its independent body, the Telecommunications Authority of Trinidad and Tobago, passed the Telecommunications Act to regulate the local telephone system, over which local telephone company the Telecommunications Services of Trinidad and Tobago had a stranglehold. As an ancillary to the act, a draft broadcast code (2004) was introduced to regulate the radio and television stations, which had grown tremendously because of deregulation and open competition and which were generally freer in the way they operated. The code specifically focused on mainstream electronic media only.

The code, among other things, provided guidelines to regulate programme content. Regarding news content, it stated that news in whatever form must be reported with due accuracy and impartiality. In terms of electoral coverage, it also stated that citizens must receive a sufficient range of information, views and opinions, as well as facts, to make well-informed choices, and that broadcasters must avoid unjust treatment of individuals or organizations.

The Broadcast Code, which was put out for public comment, received a mixed review from the Trinidad and Tobago Publishers and Broadcasters Association, which represents media owners involved in radio and television fields. The association forewarned that the main challenge of the code was how to set standards for the industry without interfering with the guaranteed freedom of expression of thought and opinion within the operation. It also stated that it was unfair to regulate only one arm of the media while ignoring the others (Trinidad and Tobago Publishers and Broadcasters Association 2009).

In 2009, One Caribbean Media Limited, the parent company of TV6 and the *Express* newspaper, recommended that the code be revisited and modified on the basis of the position raised by One Caribbean Media, which included that the authority should embrace a regulatory landscape for broadcasters that included that broadcasters themselves engage in self-regulation through internal codes of conduct, the Media Complaints Council, the courts of law and the Telecommunications Authority of Trinidad and Tobago (One Caribbean Media Limited 2009).

The code was revised several times according to consultations with various stakeholders, and in March 2014, a final draft was completed. This final draft included regulations governing broadcasting of elections on news and current-affairs programmes, and stipulated that discussion and analysis of election issues must end by midnight on the night before the opening of polling stations, that the results of any opinion polls on polling day should not be broadcast until election polls close and that broadcasts must not contain any content in which candidates and representatives acted as news presenters, interviewers or presenters of any type of programme during the election period (Telecommunications Authority of Trinidad and Tobago 2014).

Similarly, the Broadcasting Commission of Jamaica has also developed guidelines for political broadcasts for the electronic media in that country during elections, although they are not as detailed as those found in Trinidad. These include the identification of political party/sponsor and state that broadcasters must give equal airtime to all political parties and candidates. Any financial concessions made by broadcasters for airtime to a political party or candidate must also be offered in the same form to other parties and candidates (Broadcasting Commission of Jamaica 2014).

Guyana's Broadcasting Commission is somewhat vague regarding its regulations governing the electronic media. Its Act Number 17 of 2011 refers mostly to licensing arrangements, although some mention is made of accuracy, fairness and balanced reporting of news (Guyana National Broadcasting Commission 2011).

The issue at all times has been, and perhaps will continue to be, how to achieve balanced reporting and fair coverage among competing political interests, how the independence and insulation of media from undue political influence can be secured, how to make the clearest distinction between news and views and paid campaigning by special interests and finally how to manage coverage so that citizens can draw sensible conclusions and informed choices.

Regulating Electoral Campaigns in Trinidad and Tobago

Electoral campaigns, although highly mediatized, are to a large degree still unregulated in Trinidad and Tobago, with the media generally being left on their own to develop in-house guidelines for covering political campaigns. In addition, the media have been totally against any form of government intervention in their domain, even if well intentioned. In most instances, the media perceive government's intervention as an attempt to control and manipulate the free press through censorship.

The constitution of Trinidad and Tobago, the Elections and Boundaries Commission (EBC), and the Draft Broadcast Code (2014) provide some rules and regulations for conducting free and fair elections. However, not much guidance is provided by the state on media coverage of political campaigns. Sections 70–73 of the constitution provide guidelines for the registration of voters under the supervision of the EBC, the boundaries of the various constituencies and the system of balloting. However, no mention is made of media coverage of campaigns during elections.

To protect themselves from allegations of bias, in 1997, the media owners and managers of Trinidad and Tobago established a self-monitoring agency called the Media Complaints Council, which has developed its own code of practice to help maintain public trust and confidence in the news media by promoting fairness, courtesy and balance and by creating a forum where the public and the news media can engage each other in examining standards of journalistic fairness.

Further, to ensure that national elections were reported fairly by the local media, the Association of Caribbean Media Workers, in collaboration with the United Nations Educational, Scientific and Cultural Organization, or

UNESCO, developed "An Election Handbook for Caribbean Journalists" (Association of Caribbean Media 2009) to provide some guidelines to journalists covering elections. The handbook outlined guidelines for covering political campaigns in terms of fairness, reader interest, clarity and accuracy. In terms of fairness, the handbook stated, "Reporting, in words and images, must be seen to be fair and unbiased. Especially at election season, opinions must also be seen to reflect balance" (Grant and Gibbings 2009, 17). In addition, it stated that it was necessary to give exposure to all contesting parties.

Similar self-regulating mechanisms for the conduct of free and fair elections were established by the regional media in Guyana and Jamaica. In January 2006, the "Code of Conduct for the Media for Reporting and Coverage of Guyana Elections 2006 for Owners, Publishers, Editors and Journalists, including Associated Guidelines" was signed by thirty-nine media leaders in Guyana during a roundtable discussion (Guyana Elections Commission 2016). This code detailed how broadcast and print journalists should conduct themselves during elections, including not publishing and broadcasting any matter with the potential to promote or incite racial hatred, bias or contempt or that was likely to promote or cause public disorder or pose a threat to the security of the nation.

In addition, a code of ethics exists for members of the Association of Caribbean Media Workers, and Jamaica has developed its own code of conduct. Both codes have been modelled after the "Editors' Code of Practice" which was ratified by the Press Complaints Commission of the United Kingdom in 2003. In the post-2010 period, self-regulatory mechanisms were established in both Trinidad and Tobago and Jamaica for politicians to conduct themselves with integrity and for peaceful general elections. In Trinidad and Tobago, in July 2014 a number of civic groups developed "The Code of Ethical Political Conduct" for the conduct of peaceful elections which was signed by seven political parties including the PNM and the UNC. Similarly, in Jamaica, in February 2016 both the prime minister and the leader of the opposition at that time signed the Code of Political Conduct. The Jamaican code stipulates eight principles, covering non-violence and non-intimidation; safety of private and public property; avoidance of confrontation; public utterances; freedom of access; avoidance of defacing of buildings and installations; a code of ethics; and political tribalism.

Soft Control Mechanism

Successive governments have tried to find "soft" means by which to regulate the free press, and this was generally done through the introduction of legislation on which the media were given ample opportunity to comment and to be part of the process. In a situation in which freedom of the press is enshrined in the constitution, this was generally met with much antagonism. In 1997, the UNC government introduced its Green Paper "Reform of Media Law: Towards a Free and Responsible Media", in which the government tried to reform the archaic colonial laws affecting the media in Trinidad and Tobago and regulate the media by developing a code of ethics for the press. Interestingly, in attempting to reform the laws relating to media, one of the clauses would have ensured "special protection for journalists against punishment for contempt for refusing to disclose their sources of information and contempt of Parliament" (Attorney General 1997).

Ken Gordon, a former government minister under the NAR government and one of the most influential media personalities locally and regionally, who was also former chief executive officer of CCN, the parent company of the *Express,* responded on behalf of the media fraternity:

> The Green Paper is a combination of irrelevancies, such as licensing of journalists, which has never been an issue in Trinidad and Tobago, pious statements clearly designed to create a false sense of security, inaccurancies, giving assurances about clauses in the Jamaican Code of Ethics, which do not exist, and cleverly designed machination. It is philosophically wrong. Machiavellian in content and designed to insiduously [*sic*] erode one of the important checks and balances in our country. (Gordon 1999, 171)

His response resulted in a public outcry over attempts at curbing press freedom while eliciting a livid response from Prime Minister Basdeo Panday. Given the furore that resulted, the UNC gvernment was forced to withdraw the Green Paper (1997), but not before Panday displayed his displeasure and attacked Gordon publicly, accusing him of being "a pseudo-racist . . . to maintain his monopolistic advantage over his competitors in the media" (Gordon 1999, 168). A long court battle ensued in which Gordon sued Panday for libel and defamation of character. The court ordered Panday to pay Gordon more than TT$600,000 in damages.

Withholding State Advertising

However, there were other more subtle and not-too-subtle ways in which governments have tried to control the free press in this country. One of the most popular means was by starving media houses of state advertising and, in one case, of foreign currency to purchase paper for printing. The other side of this was the "bribing" of newspapers with heavy advertising. In a country in which the state is the largest advertiser, this can lead to the untimely downfall of newspapers. The *TnT Mirror*, which has a tradition of being highly critical of most governments, whether UNC or PNM, paid a heavy price for the slant, tone and content of its newspaper: in February 2012, its publisher complained that state boards had stopped advertising with it for what he termed "Cabinet's attempt to punish the newspaper for independent reporting" (*TnT Mirror*, 6 October 2012, 10). In fact, this country has been littered with newspapers that have had short life spans because of inadequate advertising revenues, such as the *Daily Mirror*, the *Probe* and the *Independent*.

Spying on Journalists

In addition, the Patrick Manning regime (2007–2010) was accused of a highly unorthodox method of spying on journalists by illegally intercepting information through wiretapping. The illegal wiretapping of phones of certain journalists, opposition politicians and prominent citizens was discovered to have been conducted by the Special Intelligence Unit, with a direct link to the Office of the Prime Minister (*Newsday*, 14 November 2010). It was also discovered that the Special Anti-Crime Unit of Trinidad and Tobago, under the aegis of the Office of the Prime Minister, was also involved in wiretapping phones as part of its routine surveillance function. In the aftermath of the 2010 election, the Interception of Communications Bill 2010 was passed in the parliament by the PP government to reduce the illegal practice of wiretapping of phones to safeguard the privacy of nationals of this country. The legislation was enacted on 17 December 2010, making illegal wiretapping punishable by a fine of TT$300,000 and five years' imprisonment (Interception of Communication Act 2010). On 10 May 2016, the PNM government successfully amended the Strategic Services Agency Act to extend the agency's mandate to operate in relation to serious crimes. This amendment, which was passed with considerable opposition both by opposition parliamentarians and senators and by the general public, gave the government the right to intercept communication by any citizen whom it deemed to be a threat to the national security of the country.

In 2012, the 2010 incident negatively affected the country's international reputation as a place in which the media enjoyed a high level of press freedom. In February 2012, Reporters Without Borders ranked Trinidad and Tobago fiftieth in its World Press Freedom Index 2011–2012, down twenty places "as a result of a scandal involving spying on journalists, as well as moves to boycott radio and television stations on procedural abuses" (Reporters Without Borders 2012). This was especially difficult for the local media's regional standing, given that Jamaica had been ranked sixteenth, far higher than Trinidad and Tobago, whereas the Organisation of Eastern Caribbean States was ranked twenty-fifth. Although the country's ranking has improved slightly over the years, to forty-first in 2015 and forty-fourth in 2016, one can surmise that this amendment will most likely have a negative effect on the country's press-freedom ranking and reputation.

Strong-Arm Tactics to Regulate the Free Press

However, by 2012, regulating the free press took a dramatic turn in this country, when a key agent of the state abandoned its soft approach and attempted to forcibly bring the press into line when it was perceived that the media had broken the law in sourcing information and publishing/airing stories. In October 2011, the police enforced the Broadcast Code to enter the CCN TV6 television station and seized a video clip of a child in the act of being raped that had been aired on one of its programmes, *Crime Watch*. This resulted in a public uproar over the heavy hand of the state and the use of strong-arm tactics in regulating media content on television. Similarly, on 9 February 2012, police from the Anti-Corruption Investigations Bureau of Trinidad and Tobago stormed into *Newsday* and seized a computer, two flash drives and two cellular phones belonging to senior investigative reporter Andre Bagoo because he refused to reveal his source of information for an article relating to the Integrity Commission. The commission insisted that it was bound by confidentiality and felt that important information was leaked to the press by one of its members. The police stated that they were acting lawfully and just doing their job as stipulated in the Integrity in Public Life Act.

Although both the attorney general, Anand Ramlogan, and Prime Minister Persad-Bissessar issued statements distancing the PP government from the incident, the damage had already been done, with perhaps the majority of citizens disbelieving that the government did not have a hand in this incident. Describing the incident as an "extreme act", Persad-Bissessar stated: "The Government believes in and respects the reporter's right to protect the source of his/her information unless it would not be in the public's interest to do so. . . . The Government reaffirms its deep commitment to the protection and preservation of the independence and freedom of the media . . . we believe in open access of information to journalists rather than obstruction of the process" (*Express*, 11 February 2012).

Both incidents introduced the use of strong-arm tactics to control the free press. Although Trinidad and Tobago has had a history of combative relationships between politicians and the local media, especially around elections, the relationship had seldom descended to the use of police force. The only previous recorded incident of the use of strong-arm tactics against the media occurred on 27 July 1990, when the radical Muslim group the Jamaat al Muslimeen stormed local television station TTT and forcibly took over the station for six days as it attempted to overthrow the democratically elected NAR government. These incidents had a deleterious effect on the psyche of the local media, accustomed to a high level of press freedom under the constitution.

The International Press Institute openly condemned the actions by the authorities and demanded an immediate apology from the commissioner of police in Trinidad and Tobago. The Press Association of Jamaica also issued a statement denouncing the actions of the police. Similar statements were issued by the Association of Caribbean Media Workers, the Trinidad and Tobago Publishers and Broadcasters Association and One Caribbean Media Limited.

Although local, regional and international press bodies were quick in defending the rights of the press in Trinidad and Tobago, the responses from civic society, nationals and other interest groups were slow in coming, if they came at all. One could discern a certain amount of cynicism towards the free press of this country by people accustomed to being at the wrong end of the jounalist's pen, with little form of redress.

Self-Regulation

The local press has always enjoyed tremendous freedom, based on section 4 of the constitution of Trinidad and Tobago, which lists freedom of the press as one of the fundamental rights of the people of the country; the Freedom of Information Act (1999), which was enacted in 2001, made it possible for any national to access information from government or its institutions. The government was also a signatory to the Chapultepec Declaration adopted by the hemispheric conference on free speech, held in Mexico City on 11 March 1994. The declaration, which listed ten principles of press freedom, was signed by Prime Minister Manning on 12 September 2002 (IAPA 1994). The Chapultepec Declaration stated that freedom of expression is an individual right of the people; every person has the right to seek and receive information, express opinions and disseminate them freely; public-sector information should be made available to journalists on a timely basis, and no journalist should be forced to reveal his or her sources; the media and journalists should neither be discriminated against nor favoured because of what they write or say; and no news media or journalist may be punished for publishing the truth or criticizing or denouncing a government.

In an environment in which the press in Trinidad and Tobago enjoyed a tremendous amount of freedom with little interference from government and the police, it was difficult to accept government censorship or control in any guise. However, the media have at their disposal their own professional organizations, in which mechanisms have been put in place for self-regulation. A Media Complaints Council was established in 1997 after the infamous Green Paper on the reform of media law specifically "to help maintain public trust and confidence in the news media by promoting fairness, courtesy and balance and by creating a forum where the public and the news media can engage each other in examining standards of journalistic fairness" (Media Complaints Council n.d.).

In addition, the media now have their own professional organization, the Media Association of Trinidad and Tobago, which represents the interest of all media workers (Media Association of Trinidad and Tobago 2006). Others include the Independent Media Producers of Trinidad and Tobago, and the Trinidad and Tobago Publishers and Broadcasters Association. They are also part of a global network in which journalism standards and regulations are taken into account. These include regional, Commonwealth and international organizations such as Canadian Journalists for Free Expression, the International Federation of Journalists, the International Press Institute, National Union of Journalists and Reporters Without Borders.

Although local professional media organizations have been established by the media to regulate the profession, these organizations seem to lack support from the media fraternity, resulting in low participation among media practitioners. In light of these developments, the professionalization of the media through the strengthening of media organizations and practitioners through training and exposure would bode well for the development of local journalism. At a time when the role of the media is being questioned and their impartiality is under scrutiny, especially during elections, it is imperative that the relevant professional organizations be strengthened to withstand public censure and politicians' perception of biased media coverage.

Restructuring Trinidad and Tobago's Media

During the period since independence, especially since 1986, the media have undergone changes in structure and ownership, expanding from foreign ownership to ownership by private individuals and large multimedia companies owned by conglomerates. Both the *Express* and the *Guardian* are subsidiaries of larger companies, the business interests of which extend into other entrepreneurial activities such as the Guardian Media Limited and CCN. The Trinidad Publishing Company had traditionally owned the *Trinidad Guardian* but has expanded into Guardian Media Limited, which includes radio and television (CNC3). The *Guardian* belongs to a privately owned family company that is publicly traded, the ANSA McAL Group of Companies, with businesses in real estate, insurance, mortgages and car dealerships throughout the region.

Similarly, the *Express* has expanded from newspaper to providing satellite (DirecTV) and national television (TV6) and radio. The *Express* is now part of a large conglomerate called One Caribbean Media, with media houses in Barbados and Grenada. The other newspapers, *Newsday, Bomb, Mirror, Catholic News* and *Tobago News*, are all owned by individuals or groups and represent the views of certain segments, religious bodies and private interest groups.

To a large extent, radio continues to be owned by private individuals and to cater for the country's diverse population through niche marketing, so that certain stations play only East Indian music and some focus mostly on religious content. Others are dedicated to local cultural content such as calypso and soca music. The state media have also been restructured along the lines of the local private media in an attempt to compete for niche markets. They have consolidated under the Caribbean News Media Group and Government Information Services. Media concentration in the hands of a few continued with the purchase of Citadel radio by One Caribbean Media in April 2012.

Ownership of media houses by large businesses also raises the issue of whether the media can truly be independent of business interests in a small country such as Trinidad and Tobago, in which the business community is relatively small and well connected, and is generally highly dependent on government support through advertising, contracts and subsidies. Conglomerates are more concerned about profit margins and the bottom line and would hardly incur the wrath of government in the name of media integrity, professionalism and ethics. Neither would they be willing to subvert good relations in their business networks by publishing information that could be harmful to their colleagues and their companies. This is especially relevant in the context of Trinidad and Tobago, in which the population is relatively small. The networks between the different sectors include deep familial ties, which make it difficult for the media to operate independently of these interests. The establishment of the central-based newspaper *Sunshine* by former politician Jack Warner, after his exit from the PP government (2010–2015), raises the issue of the independence of such a newspaper and whether it can be truly objective in its publication, given its ownership.

McChesney (1998) argued that media systems operate to serve the needs of owners, and what is most profitable for media corporations is not what is best for a democratic society; further, McChesney argued that the craft of journalism had declined because of commercial pressures. As in Latin American countries, media concentration in Trinidad and Tobago is occurring at a slower pace than in countries such as the United States, where the media are controlled by large oligopolies such as Time Warner. Further, media concentration in different political regimes has different consequences for public life (Waisbord 2002). Media concentration in a small society in which civil-society capacity is not fully developed and concentration in a large society with strong countervailing institutions can be very different.

Veteran journalist George John, in his memoirs (2002), wrote about the conflict in interest between editorial policy and ownership policy in the *Express* newspaper, which he claimed were at odds with each other during his early career. According to author and journalist Raymond Ramcharitar, this alignment to business has resulted in a pro-business bias and is demonstrated in the pro-business articles published, as well as the editorial policy of the press (Ramcharitar 2005). Similarly, Ramcharitar also recounted his experiences at the *Guardian*, in which the editor-in-chief had a regular column in the *Business Guardian*, writing specifically about businesses in the country. Ramcharitar (2005) also wrote about the disdain and contempt most people had for the local banks because of their disrespect for the way they managed ordinary citizens' accounts, stating that one hardly ever saw any negative information printed about them in the press.

This situation makes the media vulnerable to politicians, who ultimately decide who gets the largest chunk of advertising from government. The *Independent* newspaper, which enjoyed a short life span in Trinidad (1998–2001), was bought out by the *Express*, which absorbed its staff and then shut it down. The *Independent* had been starved of state advertising because it was perceived to be anti-UNC (Cruikshand 2005). The *TnT Mirror* had been subject to similar treatment by successive governments since its inception because it tended to take an opposition stance and focused on underground reporting and exposés, which are generally issues not covered by the daily press.

Movement towards Digitization of Printed Media

This situation is exacerbated by global trends and the dramatic decline in readership of hard copies of newspapers in favour of online news, making it even more difficult for newspapers to survive. As a result, many media houses have embraced new Internet technologies to achieve economies of scale to stay competitive and extend distribution to a wider spread of readers. Most of them have now converted their printed newspapers into online papers as well. The *Guardian* is available online and can be accessed on any device that links to the Internet. The newspaper has also added social-media interactivity and video streaming to its main websites. In 2015, the newspaper embarked on an automation project, using the latest Internet technologies to reduce operating costs and modernize its operations.

Similarly, the *Express* has also gone online and is available to both local and international audiences at www.trinidadexpress.com. In 1997, the newspaper registered its first digital newspaper: digital.trinidadexpress.com, which is available to online subscribers for a fee. In 2014, the group invested in digital technologies to ensure that the newspaper is available to its readers on multiple devices such as smartphones, tablets and other electronic gadgets.

Newsday has also embraced Internet technology and is available on the web at www.newsday.co.tt, although it has lagged behind somewhat in digitization of its operations when compared with the other dailies.

During 2000–2010, the mainstream media also faced competition from online blogs and social-networking sites such as Facebook. In the post-2010 period, social media, especially Facebook, have become a serious threat to mainstream media as more people use this unregulated citizens' platform to receive the latest news in real time and to air their concerns on topical issues without fear of censorship. More politicians are developing their own Facebook accounts to reach their constituents and to have their views heard. In Trinidad and Tobago, where governing parties are generally given more coverage than opposition parties by the mainstream media, the opposition has begun to use this form of media to express its opinions on national issues and to advocate for change in policies while reaching large groups of people both throughout the country and abroad. The use of social media also allows politicians to interact with both supporters and non-supporters directly.

The use of social media in political campaigning, although slow to catch on in the 2000–2010 period, has begun to grow in momentum in the lead-up to the 2015 election, and it is anticipated that it will become even more important in campaigning for young voters in future elections in Trinidad and Tobago, as was found in the United States during the Obama presidential campaigns.

More Female Journalists

The composition of staff in media houses has also gone through dramatic changes, with more women being hired in newsrooms and in senior positions. George John wrote about the lack of women in the newsroom in the 1970s at the *Trinidad Guardian* and *Express*, and about how women were "regarded as almost too precious to handle the tough assignments" (John 2002). However, over the years, female journalists have risen to the challenge and, in some instances, outnumber men in the newsroom. Many women also have held editorial positions in the press, such as Sunity Maharaj-Best of the *Express,* and in 2012, all three dailes were headed by female editors-in-chief. In addition, many female journalists have gained recognition for their work, such as investigative journalist Camini Marajh and Therese Mills, both of whom were awarded honorary doctorates from the University of the West Indies, in 2007 and 2012 respectively.

This is an important development for Caribbean media, given that global trends indicate that men continue to dominate the media profession. A survey released by the female media network group Women in Journalism on 3 March 2011 indicated that women make up only 30 per cent of all newspaper journalists in Britain, whereas men dominate political and business journalism, at 74 per cent. Gender-sensitive issues relating to women in the media profession were discussed at international fora such as UNESCO's International Programme for the Development of Communication council in March 2012 in Paris. UNESCO also concluded a gender-sensitive measurement tool for media content and staffing: "Gender-Sensitive Indicators for Media" (www .unesco.org).

Conclusion

During this period, there was a gradual transitioning away from a monopolistic state ownership of the media, as a result of the deregulation of the media system in Trinidad and Tobago. This period was also characterized by changes in the structure of media and the rise of women to the top leadership positions of press and politics. The professionalization of the journalistic field through local, regional and international networks and the media's ability to self-regulate have also been positive developments in the media. Yet the media have been consistently at odds with the state and with successive governments over control mechanisms such as censorship, while at the same time seeking to maintain balance and objectivity in the face of media concentration in the hands of a few powerful business elites. However, two positives were discerned in media and politics in Trinidad and Tobago in the post-2010 period: first, the ascendency of women to the top editorial and political positions, as was the case with the three dailies (*Express, Guardian* and *Newsday*), and the fact that the country's prime minister at that time was also a woman, and second, the continued commitment of the state to uphold the constitution as it relates to a free media has created an environment conducive to the development and growth of media and politics in Trinidad and Tobago, in spite of what might seem sometimes to be the temptation to curb and contain, and in spite of disputes between key political figures and the press and press leadership that have brewed over the years.

CHAPTER 4

Case Study of the 2000 Election in Trinidad and Tobago

IN 2000, THE UNC WON THE NATIONAL ELECTION. This was historic, as the PNM had governed the country continuously for thirty years, from 1956 to 1986, and again, from 1991 to 1995, when they were routed by an amalgam of opposition parties reconstituted as the NAR in 1985. When the dominant party in Trinidad and Tobago lost in 1995, it was the UNC that emerged to form a coalition government with NAR members from the Democratic Action Congress of Tobago. In 2000, however, the UNC began a second term, winning on its own. It was the first time that a political party led by a person of East Indian descent, Basdeo Panday, had won an outright victory at the polls. This victory was therefore historic not only because the UNC beat the PNM on its own but also because, in a country in which the two dominant political parties were rooted in competing ethnic communities, for the first time, an East Indian leader of the traditional opposition party had emerged as prime minister without having to depend on a coalition.

The UNC, after the election of 2000, became very fractious internally through a raging battle for leadership succession. This subsequently evolved into factionalism and charges against the sitting prime minister from within the party, and charges of failure to act against corruption by party members and supporters. The end result was that one year, more or less, into the second term of the UNC government, the ruling party was forced to call a fresh election. The leader of the UNC was Basdeo Panday; the leader of the opposition was Patrick Manning, who had served as prime minister from 1991 to 1995.

Campaign Period

The campaign period for the 2000 election lasted exactly thirty-nine days, from 2 November to 11 December, from the date the election was called to the day of the actual election. During that period, 117 newspapers were generated by the three dailies: the *Guardian, Express* and *Newsday*. All three newspapers are owned by the private sector and target different sectors, although much overlapping has been discerned in their distribution strategy, design and format. The *Guardian* has traditionally targeted an older and more conservative business sector within the middle- to high-income groups, the *Express* is also a business paper and targets a middle-income group, and *Newsday* targets mostly those in the working class.

Front Pages

Analysis of photos, headlines and news stories of all front pages, numbering a total of 117 issues of the *Express, Newsday* and *Guardian,* revealed that the 2000 election was covered moderately by all three newspapers, with just over 50 per cent (60 front pages) of all three newspapers published during the campaign period focused on the 2000 election. From the three newspapers, there was an average of twenty editions (51.28 per cent) during the thirty-nine-day campaign period that focused primarily on the 2000 election.

Of the three newspapers, the *Guardian* had the most front pages, at 27 (69.2 per cent), followed by the *Express*, at 21 (53.84 per cent). *Newsday* had the smallest number of front pages, at 12 (30.76 per cent). In 2000, the *Guardian's* broadsheet format was larger in size than the two tabloids and allowed more

Table 4. Front Pages for 2000 Election

Newspaper	Total Number of Front Pages Published	Number of Front Pages on Election	%
Guardian	39	27	69.23
Express	39	21	53.84
Newsday	39	12	30.76
Total	117	60	153.80
Average	39	20	51.28

space for a combination of photos, headlines and news content on its covers when compared with the other two dailies. The *Express* front pages tended to be a combination of large photos (between a quarter and full pages) with headlines, followed by the beginning of news stories. Editorial choice of front-page covers, overall interest in politics and national elections by the owners of the newspaper and general zeal by journalists for covering political campaigns are also contributing factors to the higher coverage in the *Guardian* newspaper.

Photos

Photos featured on the front pages were counted to determine the number of times opposition leader Patrick Manning and Prime Minister Panday appeared alone and how many times they appeared together on the front page of each newspaper. Further, the number of times each newspaper focused on other politicians in both political parties, instead of the two political leaders, was also taken into account.

An examination of photos on the front pages revealed that the prime minister was featured more times than the opposition leader and other politicians involved in the 2000 election. Panday appeared thirteen times alone compared with Manning, who appeared only three times in all three newspapers. However, both politicians appeared nine times together on the front covers, whereas other politicians were equally featured, appearing approximately ten times on the front covers. Although all three newspapers featured Panday either alone or with Manning, the *Guardian* and *Newsday* never featured Manning alone on the front covers, but chose to feature him together with the prime minister.

Table 5. Front-Page Photos for 2000 Election

Newspaper	Opposition Leader[*]	Prime Minister[†]	Both Politicians	Other Political Personalities (Both Parties)
Guardian	0	2	5	1
Express	3	6	2	7
Newsday	0	5	2	2
Total	3	13	9	10

[*]Patrick Manning
[†]Basdeo Panday

Headlines

Headlines were read to determine initial impression of bias, using a scale show-ing negative, positive or balanced. Evidence points to all three dailies being more objective in their publishing of headlines on the front covers of news-papers. Of a total of sixty headlines, twenty-nine (48.3 per cent), or a little less than half, were found to be objective, whereas nine (15 per cent) were positive to the UNC compared with the PNM's five headlines (8.3 per cent).

All three dailies carried more negative headlines on the UNC: eighteen (30 per cent) compared with the PNM's two (3.3 per cent). The *Express* carried the most negative headlines on the UNC: ten (16.6 per cent) compared with the PNM's one (1.6 per cent). *Newsday* had no negative headlines on the PNM on its front covers during the 2000 election.

Table 6. Front-Page Headlines for 2000 Election

Newspaper	UNC			PNM		
	+	−	B	+	−	B
Guardian	0	5	19	1	1	19
Express	5	10	6	1	1	6
Newsday	4	3	4	3	0	4
Total	9	18	29	5	2	29

News Stories (Inside Newspapers)

A sampling of news stories contained inside the newspapers were coded to determine which of the five frames of personality, issue, governing, conflict and horse-race frames were more prevalent. During the 2000 election, politi-cian-as-a-personality was the most dominant frame in news stories, with the incumbent prime minister, Basdeo Panday, being the most profiled politician when compared with the opposition leader, Patrick Manning.

Other politicians as a composite group, including individual politicians from both government and opposition, were also featured highly by all three dailies. However, the incumbent prime minister (Panday) dominated the news stories in the three daily newspapers. The second most popular frame was horse-race frame, indicating the high interest by newspapers in covering the

Table 7. Frames for 2000 Election

News paper	Number of Articles	Issue	Person-ality (Panday)	Person-ality (Manning)	Other Politician	Govern-ing	Conflict	Ho Ra
Guardian	27	122	78	54	91	—	6	2
Express	37	73	156	114	92	6	24	
Newsday	47	116	102	88	22	5	15	
Total	111	311	336	256	205	11	45	3
Average	37	103.66	112	85.33	68.33	3.66	15	12

2000 election as a contest between contending parties as they raced towards the polls. This is not unusual, given the high interest of the citizenry in national politics and the outcome of elections in a country in which, for two consecutive terms, the UNC was able to beat the PNM to govern the country. Issue frame was also used by journalists during the election, indicating general interest in issues considered to be of national importance by the media. Conflict frames did not garner much interest from journalists, indicating a deliberate attempt to sideline contentious issues between politicians and parties in favour of more substantial issues of national importance. Governing or unity frames were given the least importance in terms of framing of news, indicating the general lack of interest in this topic. One can surmise that previous attempts at unity and coalitions between parties, especially the NAR experience in 1986, had a deleterious effect on the national psyche, creating much cynicism regarding whether these attempts were genuine.

Panday was the most profiled politician in the newspapers because he was both political leader of the UNC and the incumbent prime minister of Trinidad and Tobago. He was also the first prime minister of East Indian descent in the history of Trinidad and Tobago, having wrestled power away from the PNM, whose base was mostly people of African descent. The PNM was also a party that had enjoyed power almost without interruption in the post-independence period. Panday's rise to power was historic, as he was the longest-serving leader of the opposition in the parliament. Panday also had a colourful career as a trade unionist and politician. In 1986, he walked out of the coalition govern-ment of the NAR, led by Prime Minister A.N.R. Robinson, to form his own political party, the UNC, after having a major dispute with Robinson. Even so, by 1995, when he won office, and in 2000, Panday's flair for dramatics, his charismatic style and his crafty use of phrases endeared him to the people and made him a much-sought-after politician among the media. Panday never failed to deliver drama, and it was not surprising that he was the most featured politician in all three newspapers, both on the front pages and in the news stories.

An initial reading of news stories gave the impression that all three newspapers generally strove for balance when reporting on both UNC and PNM, but the evidence pointed to a tendency among all three newspapers to use more negative frames when reporting on the UNC compared with the PNM (30:7). The *Guardian* carried no negative frames on the PNM, but was twice as positive to the PNM (table 8).

Analysis of the front pages and news stories of all three dailies indicated a strong editorial bias in favour of Panday in terms of choice of news material featured on the front covers, with Panday being the most photographed politician compared with the opposition leader. In contrast, editors exhibited more objectivity in their headlines, even though most headlines were focused on the UNC. In terms of news stories, journalists generally used "politician as a personality" as the main frame when reporting on political news, demonstrating a structural bias within the press to report mainly on the political leader of the UNC and the prime minister of the country. Most newspapers tended to feature the political party in government and the political leader because that person was responsible for developing national policy and managing the affairs of the country and because all elected governments are generally open to public scrutiny because incumbents have more to account for. However, the 2000 election-campaign coverage revealed a decided emphasis on coverage of the incumbent prime minister, Basdeo Panday.

Table 8. Bias Scale for News Stories for 2000 Election

Newspaper	UNC			PNM		
	+	–	B	+	–	B
Newsday	18	11	14	12	3	13
Express	14	10	5	6	4	5
Guardian	2	9	16	3	0	16
Total	34	30	35	21	7	34

However, although the press focused on the personalities, it was careful to stay away from personal conflicts between the leaders or their parties or conflicts within the respective parties. Of even less importance was the media's framing of elections in terms of unity, partnership and coalition. Surprisingly, during the 2000 election, the NAR was still a factor. The NAR was a coalition party that formed the government from 1986 to 1991. The UNC emerged as a breakaway party from the NAR, and by 2000, the NAR had become a shadow of its former self. From early on in the election process, the press seemed to have ruled out the NAR as a serious contender and hardly focused on that party in its election coverage. For all intents and purposes, therefore, the 2000 elections were a two-party contest between the PNM and the UNC, which had supporters from the two largest ethnic groups in the society – Africans and East Indians – respectively.

Editorials

In general, editorials in the *Express* were informative and educational, seeking to stress important issues that affect the lives of the population. These included the role of the EBC during elections, as demonstrated in an editorial entitled "A Fair Electoral Process" (5 November 2000, 16); the importance of citizens' exercising their democratic right to vote in an editorial entitled "A Single Vote Can Make a Difference" (11 November 2000, 16); and bringing to the attention of citizens corrupt acts committed under the guise of governance, as indicated in an editorial published 1 December, "The EBC Must Speak Up Now" (1 December 2000, 16). At times, editors used their editorials to bring politicians back in line, especially when they openly criticized national institutions such as the police service in editorials entitled "Politicizing the Police" (12 December 2000, 16) and "Leave the Police Out of Politics" (15 November 2000, 16); as well as the EBC for conducting its duties in an editorial entitled "A Fair Electoral Process" (5 November 2000, 16). The *Express* was especially harsh on politicians when they tried to mix politics and government during campaign periods, such as using official government functions to address schoolchildren and to speak on political issues, as in an editorial entitled "Civics Not Politics" (11 November 2000, 16). The paper was also highly protective of its role as part of a free press in guarding the country's democracy and was resentful of attacks levelled against its colleagues in the media for doing their job, as indicated in the editorial headline "Different Ball Game Here Mr PM" (10 November 2000, 16).

Newsday had editorials similar to those in the *Express*, but it varied in the tone of its language, which tended to be more pointed and opinionated on issues. Although both the *Express* and *Newsday* were generally critical of Panday, *Newsday* especially was highly resentful of Panday's style of governance and deeply suspicious of his motives as prime minister as indicated in editorials headlined "Why 24 Seats, Mr Panday?" (6 November 2010, 10) and "Possible Problems" (14 November 2010, 10) and "Making False Declaration" (24 November 2010, 10).

The *Guardian* editors focused on issues similar to those discussed by the other two dailies. However, this newspaper was more measured when referring to certain topics, highlighting national issues as they related to the citizenry of the country. It was especially concerned about the country's democracy as indicated in an editorial entitled "Electoral Democracy" (6 November 2000, 14). There was a tendency for the *Guardian*'s editors to be less critical of Panday as prime minister compared with the editors of the other two dailies, cautioning him "to watch those promises" (10 November 2000, 14), while berating Manning for tarnishing the reputation of the country in its conduct of free and fair elections, which they considered to be, as declared in an editorial, "a long step backward" (5 November 2000, 14).

Voter Padding

Voter padding was one of the key issues that were widely discussed during the 2000 campaign. During this election, the PNM accused the UNC of registering people in marginal constituencies to win the election. All three newspapers were strong in their views regarding this topic. However, they all agreed that the EBC was a reputable institution and generally conducted elections fairly. Further, they agreed that the issue of voter padding was serious and needed to be treated as such by the EBC. The editor of the *Express* insisted that the EBC should speak up on the issue of voter padding, as its handling of the matter through "stony silence . . . created fertile ground for the wildest of insinuations", and said that the EBC must live up to its reputation of "high esteem" and "integrity associated with its commissioners" (1 December 2000, 16). However, in an earlier editorial, the editor of the *Express* demonstrated his faith in the institution by using words and phrases such as "completely above board", "expression of faith", "fairness" and "no suggestion of fraud" (5 November 2000, 16) to describe the EBC's conduct of elections. The *Newsday* editor also identified the EBC with "free and fair elections" and as the "authority charged with the fair conduct of the general elections" (22 November 2000, 14). However, the editor of *Newsday* insisted there was some truth in allegations of fraudulent practices in voter padding.

In contrast, the editor of the *Guardian* viewed the allegations of voter padding by Manning as "a long step backward" (5 November 2000, 14) and condemned Manning for instilling fear in the minds of the populace. The editor indicated that this had forced Panday "to find himself between a rock and a hard place and to invite Commonwealth observers to view the election", calling this "a long step backward" in a country that was reputed for its free and fair elections and "electoral democracy" (6 November 2000, 14).

Issue of Politicizing the Police Service

The *Guardian* editor continued to focus on the nation's institutions and the role of the police service in doing its duty impartially, and especially in conducting investigations. In the editorial "Politicizing the Police" (12 November 2000, 14), he chided the UNC leader for suggesting that the police were "colluding with the opposition PNM . . . to embarrass the government" and further berated both the PNM and UNC leaders for trying to politicize the police service. In a follow-up editorial, the editor focused specifically on politician Jack Warner, scolding him for being an alarmist and for making "wild and incredible charges and sending wrong and dangerous messages" (15 November 2000, 14). The editor stated that Warner was "straining incredibility to the limits" and that he had an ulterior motive for discrediting the police and, by extension, the investigation into allegations of "voter padding" (15 November 2000, 14). This sentiment was echoed by the editor of *Newsday* in the editorial "What Is Warner's Problem?" (12 November 2000, 10). The editor of *Newsday* called Warner's statement on the police service "ill-conceived" and said it "bordered on the absurd" and had the potential of causing "immeasurable damage" (12 November 2000, 10).

In contrast, the editor of the *Guardian* sarcastically criticized the police, especially their handling of the Sumairsingh case, which the police described as "politically sensitive" (2 November 2000, 16). Hansraj Sumairsingh was a well-known chairman of a UNC regional corporation who wrote to the prime minister about being threatened by a senior UNC official. Sumairsingh was subsequently murdered in his beach house in Mayaro on the east coast of Trinidad. The police were accused of dragging their feet in the investigation, and the editor of the *Guardian* stated that although the police were proceeding with caution in their investigations, in contrast, they were acting "boldly" in carrying out their investigations into electoral-fraud charges against certain UNC ministers. He further suggested that the police were acting similarly to politicians, stating that "one way in which 'caution' was exercised was to appoint one Indo and one Afro Trinidadian to head the investigation" (12 November 2000, 16). The other was to feed the media "false information that an arrest was imminent" (12 November 2000, 16).

Issue of Dual Citizenship

Another dominant issue of the 2000 election that was addressed by the editors was the dual citizenship of two of the UNC candidates, Bill Chaitan and Winston Peters. The editor of the *Express* opined that the citizenship laws of Trinidad and Tobago were "ill-conceived" and "manipulated for ignoble purposes". Further, if "dual citizenship is permitted . . . the rights of citizenship cannot be demolished by it" and that Winston "Gypsy" Peters "deserved the opportunity to serve his people" (23 November 2000, 16). Winston "Gypsy" Peters and Bill Chaitan were both Trinidadians who held dual citizenship. The PNM felt it was constitutionally wrong for the UNC to take advantage of the ambiguity of the constitution and to send them up as representatives of the people and members of parliament. This matter was one of the most bitterly fought issues during the 2000 election.

In contrast, the editor of *Newsday* stated that Peters and Chaitan were wrong in signing false declarations in filing nomination papers, stating that it was "against the constitution for the PNM to have done it, and it is against the constitution for the UNC to do it" (24 November 2000, 10). In a further editorial, the editor indicated that the UNC's response on the filing of false nomination papers was "far from satisfactory . . . and that the UNC owes the country a full explanation" (29 November 2000, 10).

In contrast, the *Guardian's* position was that both candidates, Winston Peters and Bill Chaitan, were being discriminated against by law, using strong adjectives such as "oversight" and "absurd" (25 November 2000, 14) to describe how the laws relating to dual citizenship in Trinidad and Tobago were obscure and ambiguous.

Issue of Press Freedom

The issue of press freedom reared its head in the early part of the 2000 campaign when Panday gave an uncomplimentary response to the role the media played in the untimely and tragic death of Diana, Princess of Wales, stating that the press was inadvertently responsible for her death because of its uncontrollable behaviour. The press was incensed by Panday's insensitive comments and took offence at what it viewed as an attempt by Panday to indirectly chastise the press in Trinidad and Tobago. In general, editors shied away from attacks on political personalities, sticking mainly to the issues of governance. However, the perceived attack by Panday on the press in Trinidad and Tobago soured relations considerably, and this may well have been a defining moment for Panday in terms of his relationship with the press in 2000. In very strong and condemnatory language, the *Express* editor stated "one of the most unattractive traits of Mr Panday . . . is his readiness to make stupid statements on the assumption that his listeners are stupider" (10 November 2000, 16). The *Express* editor further wrote of "his reputation for political shrewdness being largely undeserved, and political shrewdness being in any case different from intelligence" (10 November 2000, 16). The editor openly berated Panday for being "contemptuous of the intelligence of the electorate" (10 November 2000, 16), in his uncomplimentary statements in blaming the press for Diana's death: "that her death was the kind of thing that happened when the press was not kept under control" (10 November 2000, 16) may very well have been the beginning of an escalating bad relationship between Panday and the *Express*.

Commentaries by Opinion Leaders

Columnists were fiercely critical of the Panday-led government because they felt that the UNC government was using undemocratic means, such as voter padding and the manipulation of both the constitution and the laws of the land, to win elections. Rooted in the columns was a deep fear that Panday was becoming an autocratic leader who was capable of going to extreme lengths to hold on to power. Manning was quick to capitalize on this fear by insinuating that Panday would not easily relinquish power if he were to lose the election, and so Manning introduced for the first time in the history of the country's elections the possibility that violence might be used to retain power. *Newsday* columnist and university lecturer Hamid Ghany, in exploring the possibility of "instability and transfer of power" (12 November 2000, 11) in his column, stated that "the time has come for vigilance to be exercised over our democratic traditions to protect our way of life and our institutions from the danger of civil commotion and unrest or attempts at undemocratic seizures of power". Similarly, veteran columnist George Alleyne wrote about the lack of principles in the election and condemned the UNC for trying to win elections through unfair means: "If the wholly inappropriate circumstances should succeed, and the rampart of democracy successfully stormed, what is there to stop the men and women . . . from employing other and equally immoral methods to repeatedly, access power, indeed indefinitely, and in the process whittle our freedoms, which are still guaranteed in our Constitution?" (*Newsday*, 3 December 2000, 12).

Leadership

The issue of leadership of the country was the most dominant theme that prevailed in the *Express* columns, with both the UNC and PNM leaders being the target of much discussion regarding their leadership styles. Evidence pointed to Panday's running afoul of the *Express* columnists during the 2000 election because of his wily personality, abrasive style and penchant for making acerbic comments. Panday's combative style and difficulty in accepting criticism had also contributed to his growing unpopularity among columnists such as Selwyn Ryan, whom he accused of plotting to destabilize the UNC when Ryan alleged that he had evidence from a party activist to prove that the UNC party was involved in voter padding. Selwyn Ryan was an academic and political scientist from the University of the West Indies. At the time of the 2000 election, Ryan was head of the Institute for Social and Economic Research at the university. Ryan claimed he had evidence of voter padding that was given to him by a disgruntled activist in the UNC.

Ryan had to openly defend himself against Panday's accusations, insisting he had no hidden agenda to destabilize the UNC government. It was no surprise that Ryan pronounced Panday's tenure as prime minister "an absolute disaster for the country", saying further that Panday "remained an embittered picaroon politician from the plantation". Ryan prophesied that "history will not be kind to him" (*Express*, 26 November 2000, 15). He further stated that the UNC had done little for the country and, in fact, "failed to improve its stock of moral capital" (ibid.). Columnist Raffique Shah also used harsh words to describe the UNC leader, describing him as "hypocritical" and "a dictator" with "an unimpressive track record" (*Express*, 5 and 9 November 2000, 15). Although Ryan and Shah's uncomplimentary remarks could be attributed partially to bad relations over time with the prime minister, the most damning statements came from the pen of Selwyn Cudjoe, an open supporter of opposition leader Patrick Manning and the PNM. Cudjoe directed his vitriolic rhetoric at both the prime minister and the UNC, calling them "uncivilized national crooks" and stating that the "UNC has become "ugly personified" (*Express*, 5 November 2000, 16). He further stated that "they show up their amateur, not ready-for-Prime Minister behaviour, expose the limitations of one-mannerism, and demonstrate the inherent shortcomings of money-only philosophy" (*Express*, 5 November 2000, 16).

An evaluation of the 2000 election showed that Panday, through his actions, to a large degree squandered the goodwill of the media, which were generally positive towards his government. It was unfortunate that Panday's ill-timed comment about the role of the media in the princess's death was seen as a personal attack on the media fraternity in Trinidad and Tobago, leading to strained relations between the prime minister and the media, which eventually deteriorated into an extremely hostile relationship. This is not, however, to suggest that Panday did not intend his comment to be an attack on the local media.

In an attempt to balance the anti-Panday opinion pieces, the *Express* dedicated space to several pro-UNC columnists such as Indira Maharaj and Kamal Persad, who took a more positive view of Panday's leadership as prime minister and UNC leader. Kamal Persad described Panday's leadership under the UNC as phenomenal, stating that "the Panday regime has pursued a policy of inclusion and used State resources for the advancement of the people and the progress of the country" (*Express*, 5 November 2000, 16). In a further article, he stated that Panday's "long period in politics, in government and opposition has produced a far superior leader to that of the leadership of Mr Manning" (*Express*, 10 November 2000, 16).

The opposition leader Patrick Manning also had his fair share of support-ers and detractors. Indira Maharaj wrote that Manning "has not been able to fill the leadership requirements which have now become essential for the new and altered political age". She further described him as "a grey man" who blended into the background and "inspires nothing". She continued, "His defi-ciencies in leadership have impacted negatively on the PNM. In a time when leadership at all levels of the party is critical, he is not able to bring new and innovative blood into the party" (*Express*, 1 December 2000, 17). Kamal Persad compared Manning's performance with that of the UNC leader, implying that Manning came up short on performance as a political leader because of his "vague vision" and unimpressive track record (*Express*, 5 November 2000, 16). Even Selwyn Ryan and Raffique Shah hinted that Manning's leadership did not inspire the populace. Ryan implied that Manning was not a dynamic and charismatic leader, like both the PNM's founding father, Eric Williams, and the UNC leader, Basdeo Panday, stating that "Mr Manning's coattails are fragile and cannot pull along candidates who given their own limitations, need the 'bounce' that leadership can give" (*Express*, 3 December 2000, 15). Manning was also chastised for tarnishing the reputation of the Trinidad and Tobago EBC and its reputation for the conduct of free and fair elections by implying that violence might ensue should the UNC lose the elections, and for being insensitive to the Muslim community by setting the date of the elections in the holy month of Ramadan. In contrast, commentators generally shied away from openly complimenting Manning on his leadership of the PNM. Articles in the three newspapers revolved mainly around the PNM party and what it had achieved over the years.

The press was also critical of the leadership style of Manning, although not to the extent that they were of Panday. *Newsday* in particular appeared to be more partial towards Manning than the other two newspapers. The general consensus was that Manning did not possess the charisma of his predecessor, Eric Williams, nor, for that matter, that of Panday, because of his lacklustre style. He did not sustain the interest of the media to any great extent, except in his capacity as opposition leader, and in general, when he did something wrong, the media were quick to point it out. The media, except for those columnists who were openly supportive of the PNM, were reluctant to endorse Manning as an alternative prime minister and political leader of the PNM. This disconnect between the PNM leader and his party escalated into growing disenchantment by the party faithful with Manning and, by the time of the 2010 election, would be considered one of the main reasons for the PNM's losing that election.

Race and Ethnicity

Race had always been one of the focal, yet understated, points of most elections in Trinidad and Tobago, with both parties, the PNM and UNC, representing almost equal numbers of Africans and Indians respectively. In 2000, the rhetoric of race was not discussed as extensively, with most politicians and political analysts being very careful with their choice of words and each doing everything possible to woo people from both ethnicities to join their party. Each party, in turn, continued to espouse the rhetoric of unity during election times, in the hope of attracting more people outside their traditional supporters and having a party more representative of the multiracial composition of the country. In general, race talk during elections was treated with much sensitivity and hardly ever degenerated into open ethnic conflict, as found in other societies outside the Caribbean.

The issue of race was raised by Kamal Persad, who alluded to the UNC being more "broad-based" and moving "to embrace and attract other groups and interests in the society" (*Express*, 19 November 2000, 16). This was disputed by Keith Smith, who attended both the UNC and PNM rallies in 2000, and who stated, "There were fewer Indians in the Square than there were blacks at Mid-Centre Mall even if there were no UNC jerseys and UNC posse as there were PNM jerseys and indeed, visible and circumspect PNM posse" (*Express*, 13 November 2000, 17). Kamal Persad further stated that the PNM had engaged in mere tokenism in including a few "PNM Indians" and, in the case of Nafeesa Mohammed, "a child of the PNM", in the party. In a later commentary, he further stated that the PNM had marginalized the Muslim community and had included Indians to give it an "Indian image . . . to act as brokers for their communities" (*Express*, 3 December 2000, 16). Keith Smith makes a similar analogy in terms of the UNC: "The team with the acquisition of the high-profile Jack Warner, [Winston 'Gypsy' Peters] and the out-of-the country Carlos John, was presented as reflecting the 'rainbow that is real'" (*Express*, 6 November 2000, 17). Ryan broached the topic of race when he indicated that the UNC's experience was good for the country: "[I]t had long been assumed that 'creoles' were ordained to rule this country forever. Many Indo-Trinidadians, in their state of alienation, had come to the belief that 'creoles' could not govern efficiently and effectively, and that they were corrupt. Their corresponding belief was that standards of good governance and public morality would improve if Indo-Trinidadians were given a turn at the 'karmic crease'." Ryan's highly opinionated comment was that "experience has proved otherwise" (*Express*, 21 November 2000, 15).

Ethics and Morality in Public Office

One of the main themes addressed by the *Guardian* was ethics and morality in high office, especially the conduct of individuals within political parties. Bukka Rennie, in his *Guardian* column, condemned the allegations of voter padding directed at the UNC, and especially the role of the prime minister in the fiasco. With a pun on "honourable", he waded into Panday for encouraging his supporters to "lend support" in areas where they were not so strong. The double entendre in "support" implied that there were many ways in which support could be lent and that Panday's supporters saw nothing wrong in "lend[ing] a hand", which Rennie said was tantamount to lending "an index finger". Rennie condemned this action in the strongest language, using phrases such as "low level of moral existence by so few" to describe the UNC government and further stating that it lacked "honesty, decency, morality in public affairs". He further stated that voter padding was akin to an attack on the democracy of Trinidad and Tobago. He then took his analogy one step further by linking it to the UNC, suggesting that voter padding had to do with race, ethnicity and self-preservation "to bring their kind to the fore" (*Guardian*, 29 November 2000, 15).

Tony Fraser also wrote about the lack of ethics and morality among politicians, especially the UNC. Similarly to Bukka Rennie, he too used generalizations to drive his point home. Without pointing fingers at anyone in particular, he stated that political leaders "send signals through their own political behavioural patterns that say in politics anything is acceptable once the ultimate goal of political mileage is achieved" (*Guardian*, 23 November 2000, 15). Further, he stated that, "without principle and acceptable behaviour in politics, our leaders are taking us to perdition". He then used descriptions such as "vulgar deceptions", "organized political banditry" and "smart men politicians" to show his disapproval of voter padding. He too linked this act of corruption to race "to preserve ethnic and cultural supremacy, one over the other".

Overand Padmore, a former PNM minister and a supporter of the PNM, examined integrity in the context of corruption and lack of transparency in procurement practices and accounting in government in an article entitled "More Honest Accounting Needed" (*Guardian*, 12 November 2000, 17). He stated that "corruption is not limited to dishonest financial manipulation but the unmasking of a well-developed plan to pad the electoral lists, thereby undermining their integrity". Padmore stated that the UNC government was corrupt and called for transparency and accountability in its activities. In another article, he raised the issue of the integrity of the system of governance. He viewed voter padding as "a diabolical plan to steal the election by persons at the highest level with highly developed conspiratorial minds" (*Guardian*, 5 November 2000, 17).

Analysis of Front Pages, News Stories, Editorials and Commentaries

In 2000, the press was mainly concerned about the outcome of the election and which party would emerge as the winner. Because a two-party contest has been the norm in Trinidad and Tobago, and traditionally the dominant parties have been the PNM and the UNC, the press focused on the two contending parties and viewed the election as a fiercely fought contest between them. In this context, the personality of the leaders was important. National issues were moderately reported on, with the press less interested in serious issues of governance that affected the nation, such as healthcare, education and security, to name a few. These important issues did not seem to capture media interest, which was turned to the electioneering process and the leadership of political parties. Much more in focus were the colourful personalities of the political leader of the UNC Basdeo Panday and his opponent Patrick Manning, the political leader of the PNM. The tendency for the press to presidentialize and personalize elections by focusing on leadership of political parties is an international trend in election coverage around the world, and likewise in Trinidad and Tobago, the local press focused heavily on the political leaders of the main parties.

The evidence based on analysis of the editorials of the three dailies during the 2000 election demonstrated that editors of the three newspapers were mostly concerned about issues relating to governance and adherence to the laws of the country, rather than with the various personalities involved in political parties. However, when the dailies did refer to political personalities, Panday was featured more often and less favourably than the opposition leader, Patrick Manning. The media were especially harsh on Panday because they felt that he was leading the country down the wrong path by exploiting the ambiguity of the constitution to get his own way. It did not help that Panday incited antagonism towards himself and his government by openly criticizing the media. However, there is little supporting evidence that the media had any hidden agenda to bring down the UNC government, as charged by Panday during the 2000 campaign. In fact, during the 2000 election, there was evidence that the media exhibited a certain degree of goodwill towards the government and tried to be even-handed and objective when reporting on governance issues.

Manning was also not immune to the editors' pen, as found in the pages of the *Guardian*. Manning was criticized for his lacklustre leadership style of the PNM and his myopic view in reading unholy motives into everything that the government did. The press also chided him for implying that the UNC would not easily relinquish power if it were to lose the election. In the electoral history of Trinidad and Tobago, no government has ever resisted the will of the people. On both counts, editors were harsh on Manning, as they felt that as an experienced politician and former prime minister, he should not tarnish the country's reputation for conducting free and fair elections, either within or outside the region. The editorial indicated that it was an affront to the country for Manning to suggest that a Commonwealth observer mission should be requested to observe the conduct of general elections. They were also unforgiving of Manning's attempt to politicize religion, as demonstrated in the *Newsday* editorial "Fury in Ramadan" (1 November 2000, 10), and for insinuating that Trinidad and Tobago might resort to violence in transitioning from one government to another when election results were announced. Manning had stated that Panday was wrong to call an election during the holy month of Ramadan, when Muslims celebrate Eid-al-Fitr. Further, he suggested that the UNC government would not easily give up power if it should lose. This type of action was unheard of in the history of elections in Trinidad and Tobago. However, editors were still less concerned with Manning and the PNM than with Panday and the UNC. This may very well be a trend of most editorials: to focus on the regime that holds the government and to make the leaders of the government responsible and accountable to the nation for their period of governance. In this context, within the framework of an election campaign, incumbency carries its own set of challenges.

Columnists of all three newspapers explored similar themes during this election. However the overriding issue concerned the safeguarding of the democratic rights of citizens, as enshrined in the constitution of Trinidad and Tobago. Trinidad and Tobago is a relatively young democracy, with a tradition of free and fair elections. The country also had a history of peaceful elections, with easy transitions from one administration to another. Freedom of the press was considered essential in the creation of a healthy democracy and in maintaining checks and balances among the power brokers in government and society. It was a role jealously guarded by journalists in the conduct of their duties. Although it was possible to discuss alignment of the views of some of the columnists with certain editorials in the three dailies, it is also important to emphasize their forms or issues. Moreover, it was important also to take into account that the newspapers themselves, to guard against partisan, biased columnists, took care to introduce multiple points of view in their newspapers.

Conclusion

In 2000, the media exhibited tremendous idealism in the way they viewed the society and their role as journalists. They were very protective of the country's democratic traditions and the requirements for good governance. Leaders were expected to be full of integrity, ethically sound and morally upright citizens whose actions could be held up to public scrutiny. This idealism was manifested in censure towards any politician who tried to take the country down the wrong path through corrupt practices, and in the fear of autocratic leadership in government and any hint of the use of violence to stay in power. The media were careful not to upset the society and to maintain balance by not overly focusing on race and personal conflicts, and they generally frowned on politicians who tried to use the race card to score political points.

In general, the media saw themselves as "watchdogs of democracy". Freedom of the press is enshrined in the constitution of Trinidad and Tobago and was jealously guarded by the press as its right to report on what was happening, especially during political campaigns. As the fourth estate, the press felt that its role was to maintain the balance of power by putting checks in place to ensure the smooth governance of the country. In doing their jobs, the media were viewed as being antagonistic by those politicians who became the targets of attention and censure. Although there was a tendency for certain partisan columnists to be biased in their views towards political parties and personalities, these views were generally not representative of the views of the particular newspaper in which their columns were featured. Most times, the editorials of all three newspapers were objective, reporting on governance issues while staying away from personal attacks on any one political personality. A review of the commentaries by political analysts during the campaign period indicated that the newspapers tried to be even-handed in presenting varied views from people who were academically knowledgeable, as well as the views of those openly supportive of both the UNC and the PNM. The rhetoric used by a few political extremists did border on vitriol at times; however, these columns were generally fewer in number, with editors trying to present the views of supporters of both political parties side by side, sometimes on the same page. However, the analysis disclosed that there was a structural bias in favour of Panday by all three newspapers in the choice of news reported and featured both on the front pages and inside the newspaper, by journalists and in the volume of coverage. It may well be the natural choice of all three papers to feature the political leader and prime minister of the country, as he was responsible for making policy decisions for the country. There was little evidence to show partisan bias by the *Express*, *Newsday* or *Guardian* newspapers during the 2000 campaign towards any political party or leader, and both Panday and Manning were targets of censure during the campaign.

CHAPTER 5

Case Study of the 2001, 2002 and 2007 Elections in Trinidad and Tobago

THE YEARS 2001, 2002 AND 2007 WERE CHARACTERIZED by major eruptions in the political landscape of Trinidad and Tobago. These eruptions included three elections in seven years, with two being called within less than one year of each other, long before the second election was constitutionally due; the fall of the UNC government on the basis of a technicality within one year of office; and the formation of new political parties: Team Unity and COP, which, although they did not win seats in parliament, were able to take away considerable support from the governing UNC, weaken its political base and undermine its prospects of regaining the government. This was also a period of much infighting among party loyalists, with challenges for leadership positions both in the PNM and UNC, including the emergence of a female contender within the latter. For the first time in the history of local politics, gender became a major factor in internal party elections, especially within the male-dominated UNC party. It was also a time of authoritarian leadership, with accusations of "creeping dictatorship" as the political leaders of both parties tried to stave off leadership challenges to hold on to office. The press was, as perhaps expected, at the centre of these unfolding events. For the media, caught between contending politicians and turbulence in the traditional political parties, these were heady times in which protecting their constitutional rights as a free press while maintaining a watchful eye over the country's young democracy became a core issue. In addition, the risk of being accused of bias was high, and the deterioration in relations between media and politicians began to escalate.

The 2001 election was called less than one year after the 2000 election, on 10

October, and resulted from a major falling-out between Prime Minister Panday and his deputy political leader, Ramesh Lawrence Maharaj, over allegations of corruption within the UNC party. Maharaj was also attorney general at the time. Panday's unwillingness to address corruption matters resulted in three top UNC officials, Ramesh Lawrence Maharaj, Trevor Sudama and Ralph Maraj, walking out of the UNC party and government to form a new political party called Team Unity. This group also formed an informal alliance with the opposition PNM, swaying the balance of power in parliament towards the opposition and forcing Panday to call an early election. The 2001 election ended in a tie, with the UNC and PNM parties gaining eighteen seats each. The decision of the then-president A.N.R. Robinson to hand over the government to the PNM instead of the incumbent UNC, based on the need for "morality in high office" and "spiritual values", did not sit well with supporters of the UNC, and less than ten months into office, Prime Minister Manning, faced with a hung parliament, was forced to call a fresh election on 28 August 2002. This election resulted in a clear majority for the PNM, and the party was able to govern the country for the next five years. By the time the election was called in 2007, a third party, the COP, had emerged as the result of a major fight between the leader of the UNC and his anointed successor, Winston Dookeran. Similarly to Team Unity, this party (COP), although gaining considerable support, was not able to win a seat in parliament; however, it did become a viable force in the politics of Trinidad and Tobago and, in 2010, was part of the coalition of parties under the PP brought together to form the government of the country. Team Unity, in contrast, disappeared from the political landscape of Trinidad and Tobago.

Number of Front Pages Relating to Elections

During the three campaign periods (2001–2007), an average of 52.5 per cent or just above a half of all coverage on the front pages of the *Guardian*, *Express* and *Newsday* was on the three elections. There was an average of nineteen front-page stories per newspaper, based on an average campaign period of thirty-six days.

Of the three campaign periods, 2002 carried the most front pages, with sixty-eight front pages, representing an average of 22.66 per cent per newspaper over the campaign period. The *Guardian* especially focused heavily on politics

74   MEDIATIZED POLITICAL CAMPAIGNS

Table 9. Number of Front Pages Appearing in *Express*, *Guardian* and *Newsday*

Year and Newspaper	Campaign Period (Days)	Number of Front Pages	%
2001			
Express	30	13	43.3
Guardian	"	18	60.0
Newsday	"	12	40.0
2002			
Express	39	16	41.0
Guardian	"	32	82.0
Newsday	"	20	51.3
2007			
Express	38	16	42.0
Guardian	"	27	71.0
Newsday	"	16	42.0
Total	321	170	472.6
Average	35.6	18.9	52.5

on its front pages, with 82 per cent of its publications featuring issues relating to the election in 2002.

Throughout the three campaign periods, the *Guardian* tended to focus more highly on the elections on its front covers, with an average of 71 per cent when compared with 42 per cent for the *Express*, and 44 per cent for *Newsday*. As a broadsheet, the *Guardian* was larger in size and allowed more space on the cover for a combination of news stories, photos and headlines. Both the *Express* and *Newsday* were tabloids, with their covers mostly comprising large photos and headlines with little copy, which was continued within the newspapers.

Overall, there was significant increase in political coverage on the covers of all three newspapers from 2001 to 2007, increasing from 14 per cent per newspaper in 2001 to 23 per cent per newspaper in 2002, and to 20 per cent per newspaper in 2007.

The campaign periods between 2001 and 2002 were especially tumultuous periods for politics in Trinidad and Tobago and had wider implications for governance of the country. As the fourth estate, the media were keenly interested in developments in the country's politics as they unfolded. Evidence suggested that one of the concerns of the media was how to guard the country's democratic traditions. Development in politics was viewed as important to the development of the country and was given precedence over most other events occurring during the campaigns.

Front Page Photos Featuring Political Leaders and other Politicians

The statistics on the front-page photos indicated that all three newspapers generally preferred to feature photos of other politicians from both the PNM and UNC than the two political leaders on their front covers. Other politicians were featured approximately eight times on average per newspaper during the campaign periods, more than the political leader of the UNC and the leader of the PNM, either together or alone.

The newspapers also tended to be fair to both political leaders, in terms of profiling them on the front pages. Basdeo Panday appeared on average 2.2 times, and Patrick Manning 2.1 times. There was only slight variation in the number of times both Manning and Panday appeared together, an average of 2.4 times compared with the number of times they appeared alone. The newspapers also featured to a lesser extent the political leaders of two of the dissident parties, the COP and Team Unity: Winston Dookeran and Ramesh Maharaj respectively. In some instances, some of the newspapers did not feature Manning at all on their front covers.

In 2001, Manning was never featured alone in the front covers of the *Express* and *Guardian*, and was only featured once by *Newsday*, during the entire period. During this time, the sitting prime minister, Panday, was the centre of media attention because he was responsible for governance of the country and viewed by the media as the single most important source of government information. As a result, events surrounding the prime minister, especially those related to policy decisions, overshadowed all other events. In addition, prime ministers have at their disposal a range of communications professionals such as public-relations and marketing experts, as well as consultants and advisers, who would generally ensure that ample media coverage was given to the prime minister daily.

This picture changed dramatically in 2007, when Manning was highly

Table 10. Front Page Photos for 2001, 2002 and 2007 Elections

Year and Newspaper	Both Panday and Manning	Panday Alone	Manning Alone	Other Politician	Other Parties
2001					
Express	4	4	–	7	5[*]
Guardian	1	2	–	4	3[*]
Newsday	2	2	1	3	
2002					
Express	4	2	1	6	
Guardian	2	1	2	1	
Newsday	2	1	–	6	
2007					
Express	3	4	5	18	
Guardian	3	2	6	16	
Newsday	1	2	4	10	2[†]
Total	22	20	19	71	10
Average	2.4	2.2	2.1	7.8	1.1

[*]Team Unity

[†]COP

featured on the front covers of all three newspapers as prime minister of the country. During this period, there was heightened media attention around the political campaigns because the race had become a three-way one, with the COP gaining considerable momentum in the lead-up to the national election. Manning, as the incumbent prime minister, was viewed as the person to be defeated by the COP to effect change and to make way for a new era of government.

Also, Manning was faced with leadership challenges by both his chairman and a deputy political leader, which played out in the public domain, generating sensational headlines for the dailies. Panday, whether in government or the opposition, was constantly embroiled in conflicts, and therefore was consistently featured on the front covers by all three newspapers during the campaign periods.

In general, when the press focused on one political leader, it was at the expense of the other. For example, in 2001, the newspapers hardly focused on

Manning while featuring Panday on the front pages. Panday was then prime minister, having won nineteen of the thirty-six seats in the 2000 election and becoming the first prime minister of East Indian descent in the country's history. In 2002, when Manning appeared to be a strong contender for prime minister and Panday's popularity had waned considerably, the opposition leader was featured almost the same number of times as the prime minister on the covers of newspapers. That election resulted in Manning's being victorious at the polls. He governed the country up to 2010, when an early election was called.

However both the *Express* and *Guardian* featured the political leader of Team Unity, Ramesh Lawrence Maharaj, more than the political leaders of both the UNC and PNM because of the controversies resulting from the political infighting among the leadership of that party. These fights played out publicly, under the full scrutiny of the media, and created sensational headlines and stories for all three newspapers. Moreover, Ramesh Maharaj, who had gained a reputation as a controversial human-rights lawyer outside of politics, continued to attract media attention because of his anti-government position while in government and because of the unpredictability of his actions and the implications for the governing party. Although Maharaj's defection from the UNC was a catalyst in forcing Panday to call an early election, which resulted in the fall of the UNC government in 2001, he was not able to gain a seat during the 2001 election. By 2002, Team Unity was no longer a factor in Trinidad and Tobago's politics, having disappeared from the political landscape.

In 2007, a reverse pattern was discerned, with the press instead focusing highly on Manning, as prime minister, while paying little attention to Panday, with Manning emerging victorious at the polls on 5 November 2007. However, the COP's political leader, Winston Dookeran, was placed on the front covers of *Newsday* on several occasions (table 10). The COP, like Team Unity, arose as a result of a conflict with the leadership of the UNC. However, the COP was able to attract considerable support from the population, becoming a strong third party in 2007. The COP, under the relatively untarnished leadership of Winston Dookeran and his brand of "new politics", was considered to be an attractive political alternative to the status quo, represented by the two established parties; this catapulted him into the media limelight as the most likely person to move the country forward and beyond the traditional parties. Although he was able to gain 22.64 per cent of the national votes and followed closely on the heels of the UNC, which had 29.73 per cent of the national votes, the COP was not able to win a seat in government. The PNM emerged victorious, with 45.85 per cent of the votes, winning twenty-six of the forty-one seats in parliament. The emergence of two political parties proved costly to the UNC and facilitated the consolidation of the PNM.

More Balanced Headlines on Front Pages

All three newspapers had more balanced headlines on their front covers than positive or negative headlines on the UNC or PNM over the course of the three campaign periods (table 11). This was directly related to the newspapers' tendency to lean towards featuring other politicians from both political parties, apart from the prime minister and the opposition leader, on the covers of their newspapers. Other politicians included people from within the two established parties, as well as those from the newer political parties. The large number of balanced headlines demonstrated professionalism in the editing process and the selection of newsworthy items in attracting readership. Even though editors presented their readership with what they wanted to read while appeasing the politicians, they consciously did not facilitate the hogging of the limelight by the two traditional political parties and their leaders: Basdeo Panday of the UNC and Patrick Manning of the PNM.

Negative Headlines

During the three campaign periods, the UNC had a total of thirty-seven negative headlines compared with eighteen for the PNM (table 11), indicating that all three newspapers were inclined to be more negative towards the UNC than the PNM. While in government, the UNC had attracted considerable negative publicity because of the infighting among its membership, epitomized by a leadership struggle and persistent allegations of corruption and public scandals. Many of these issues continued to haunt the UNC even while out of office. A public battle between Panday and the media also ensued, which created a hostile environment between the press and the UNC leadership; for example, the media distrusted Panday's attempt at constitutional reform, viewing it as yet another ploy by Panday to hold on to government. The number of negative headlines on the UNC averaged around 4.1 per newspaper compared with the PNM's 2.0.

Table 11. Bias Scale for Front Pages for 2001, 2002 and 2007 Elections

Year and Newspaper	PNM		UNC		Balanced
	+	–	+	–	
2001					
Express	1	1	4	1	5
Guardian	1	0	1	2	7
Newsday	2	0	2	4	3
2002					
Express	1	1	0	8	6
Guardian	1	1	1	–	8
Newsday	1	1	1	8	9
2007					
Express	3	8	3	6	8
Guardian	1	5	1	4	12
Newsday	6	1	1	3	5
Total	17	18	14	37	63
Average	1.8	2.0	1.5	4.1	7.0

In terms of positive headlines, there were fourteen positive headlines on the UNC compared with the PNM's seventeen, indicating a certain amount of objectivity and equity in the way the media portrayed both political parties and indicating that the negativity towards the UNC was mostly generated by the negative occurrences within the party and membership during its term of government, and not necessarily as a result of biased reportage. Negative news arising out of party infighting in the UNC cannot be blamed on the media, whose job was primarily to report the news as it unfolded. Reports of ongoing conflict between the prime minister and media houses cannot be blamed either.

However, the suspicion of the press about Panday's motives, in the circumstances, has to be acknowledged as being reasonable. Fourteen possible headlines for the UNC as opposed to seventeen for the PNM seemed remarkable when taking into account the striving for objectivity and balance practised by the press.

Positive Headlines

In 2001, there were more positive headlines on the UNC on the front covers, but by 2007, they had twice as many positive headlines on the PNM (table 10). In 2000, the UNC had considerable goodwill from the population and from the media which continued up to 2001, before the calling of an early election. The media reflected public perception, feelings and opinions of the people at that time. When the fortunes of the UNC became adverse in terms of national support, this was reflected in the newspapers' public profiling. The fact that, on average, they tended to be almost equally positive towards both the PNM and UNC, at 1.8 per cent and 1.5 per cent respectively, supports the argument that the media generally strove to be objective in their coverage of both political parties.

News Stories

Politicians-as-political-personalities was the most dominant theme used by the press to frame the elections. Overall, the dailies focused more on other politi-

Table 12. Coding of News Stories for 2001, 2002 and 2007 Elections

Year and Newspaper	Issue	Panday	Manning	Other Politicians	Govern-ing	Con-flict	Horse Race
2001							
Express	152	330	114	764	19	3	97
Guardian	212	155	109	592	6	4	81
Newsday	159	294	112	834	2	8	160
2002							
Express	113	94	89	155	7	48	90
Guardian	195	49	60	143	16	46	79
Newsday	150	68	109	241	18	38	122
2007							
Express	44	75	109	469	21	81	74
Guardian	63	64	178	502	35	51	34
Newsday	45	53	37	206	2	17	26
Total	1,133	1,182	917	3,906	126	296	763
Average	125.9	131.3	101.9	434.0	14.0	32.8	84.7

cians when compared with the two political leaders, even though these leaders continued to generate considerable media attention, both negative and positive.

Issue frame was the second most common one used by the media, but this was comparatively lower when compared with the politician as personality frame. The horse-race frame received an average amount of coverage, which was surprising, considering it received the second highest frame in the 2000 election. The conflict and governing frames were low in the rankings, with the latter hardly being used at all.

Politician-as-Personality Frame

The personality frame was the most widely used frame by reporters during the 2001, 2002 and 2007 elections. During the three elections, incumbent prime ministers continued to take centre stage in the media as the main sources of information: Panday in 2001 and Manning in 2002 and 2007. When these leaders became opposition leaders, they did not generate the same interest in the media; however, the media focused heavily on other politicians, especially those political leaders who emerged during the 2001 and 2007 elections. During these two elections, there were major fallings-out in the UNC, resulting in the formation of two new political parties: Team Unity, headed by Ramesh Maharaj, and the COP, led by Winston Dookeran. The new parties became third parties, and the interest generated by them suggested that the quest for new leadership and new politics was more representative of the diverse population of Trinidad and Tobago at a time when politics had reached a deadlock in terms of leadership and governance.

The heavy focus on the personality frame in the period from 2001 to 2007, with less attention paid to issues, horse-race, conflict and governing frames, indicated that the media were concerned about the leadership of the country in a situation in which both the prime minister and the opposition leader had fallen short of expectations. In 2001, Ramesh Maharaj appeared to be a potential leader under Team Unity, but the controversial circumstances under which he emerged created considerable distrust among certain elements of the society, especially the East Indian community, which blamed him for the fall of the UNC government. Similarly, the African community had also grown distrustful of him. These were some of the reasons it was difficult for him to emerge as a national leader.

In 2007, although the COP leader, Winston Dookeran, seemed an ideal candidate, he was not able to inspire and win over large segments of the population because of his lacklustre style and his perceived indecisiveness as a leader; he also presented a less charismatic figure when compared with other political leaders. The media framed those personalities who they felt were most likely to emerge as leaders of the country in a situation in which the two traditional parties had had their fair chance at governance and had stymied the political system with their brand of leadership. The dailies were less concerned about which party actually won the elections; the issues they were using to leverage national support; superficial attempts at unity and coalition; and internal conflicts. However, they were very interested in those political personalities involved in the election process and in the most likely candidate to move the country forward.

Issue Frame

Issue frames were the second most common used by journalists to frame the three elections. However, the wide disparity between personality and issue frames indicated moderate to low interest in issues of governance overall. Issues were framed on average 126 times during the three campaign periods. In general, there was a steady decline in interest in issues, with a more pronounced decline in 2007. The general lack of interest in issues was reflective of the disruptive and volatile state of politics during the 2001, 2002 and 2007 elections. The society was more concerned about the stability of governing parties and the search for new leadership at a time when corruption was rife and both the media and citizenry were disenchanted with the current leadership and parties.

Some of the issues that were reported on in 2001 included corruption by high-ranking UNC officials while in government; the Piarco Airport scandal, relating to the disappearance of a TT$50 million cheque; and the role of the EBC in voter padding and the conduct of elections.

In 2002, the country was gripped by two major scandals: the charging of Panday for not declaring a secret bank account in London during his stewardship as prime minister, and Manning's meetings with the Jamaat al Muslimeen, the radical Muslim group that had led an attempted coup in 1990 against the elected government, which was the NAR at that time.

The scandal of the huge bank account holding TT$52 million and owned by UNC minister Carlos John was also the subject of media attention during that period. In 2007, the issues reported included leadership challenges within the PNM and the UNC. Corruption and scandal talks were hardly reported on during the 2007 election; however, the negative publicity received by Panday and members of his cabinet in 2001 and 2002 over allegations of corruption would indelibly brand his government as corrupt, negatively affecting his chances of becoming prime minister again. It would also weaken his own leadership within the UNC and create the conditions for new leadership of the party to emerge.

Horse-Race Frame

During the three campaign periods, the press was moderately concerned about the contest between contending political parties and which party was likely to emerge victorious at the polls. Among the frames used by journalists, the horse-race frame was featured an average eighty-six times. Of the three dailies, *Newsday* was more focused on horse-race framing, with its interest peaking in 2001 and declining drastically in 2007. In general, *Newsday* tended to focus more on news stories rather than commentaries because of the nature of that newspaper and the market it targeted. Both the *Guardian* and *Express* were steady in their use of the horse-race frame, although there was declining interest in 2007.

This suggested a declining interest in politics among media practitioners, who were growing tired of the rapidity with which elections were being called, as three elections were held within three years, when elections were democratically planned for once every five years. It also demonstrated the growing cynicism towards politicians and political process by the media. The interchanging of two political parties between government and opposition under the Westminster system created a deadlock in national politics, stymieing the growth and development of politics. Third parties, although offering a solution to this problem, did not garner enough support from the populace, as demonstrated by their inability to win seats during elections.

Conflict Frame

Conflict frame was not as widely reported by journalists when compared with personality and issue frames. In 2001, all three newspapers showed very little interest in conflicts between politicians from the ruling and opposition parties and within political parties; however, this interest increased steadily during the campaigns of 2002, when both the PNM and the UNC were facing leadership challenges within their respective parties. It was also a period in which Panday and the press were engaged in hostile relations. In 2007, interest in conflicts peaked in the *Express*, whereas the *Guardian*'s interest plateaued and *Newsday*'s interest also declined somewhat.

In 2001, one of the major conflicts that engaged media attention concerned the fight between Panday and his attorney general, Ramesh Maharaj, over allegations of corruption within the UNC. Maharaj and two other senior members of the government, walked out of the government and formed their own party, Team Unity. This conflict spilled over to a legal battle for the party's symbol, the rising sun. Maharaj lost the battle in the courts, and Panday was able to retain his party's symbol. In 2006, conflict also arose between Panday and another senior member of his party, Winston Dookeran, over leadership of the UNC, with Dookeran walking out of the party to form the COP. There were also conflicts between Panday and two other members of the party: Persad-Bissessar and Jack Warner, regarding succession issues within the UNC. During this period, the relationship between the media, especially the *Express*, and Panday had deteriorated considerably. The negative framing of Panday through the use of the conflict frame was mainly a result of the number of conflicts he was engaged in with senior members of his party, especially those who challenged his leadership of the UNC. The conflict was intensified when it included elements of the media. In both the 2001 and 2007 elections, conflicts within the UNC contributed to loss of party support, and ultimately loss of elections. In 2001, the UNC tied with the PNM in a deadlock of eighteen seats each, and the incumbent UNC lost the government; in 2007, the PNM defeated the UNC with a clear majority.

In 2007, the major conflict reported on in the PNM concerned the public fight between Manning and his deputy political leader, Ken Valley, in which Valley accused Manning of having dictatorial tendencies, after Valley was rejected by the political leader as the party representative for his constituency.

Although Manning was framed somewhat negatively by the press, it did not affect his party's support and chances at government, as he recaptured the government for a second term in office, with a huge majority of twenty-six seats over the UNC's fifteen.

Although the media's handling of the conflict frame during these three elections demonstrated restraint, this frame was magnified when it focused on political leaders and leadership challenges within political parties, casting them in a negative light. This is not to suggest that these leaders, through their actions, did not cause them to be showcased unfavourably in the press. One can conclude that the severity of in-party fighting can lead to defection of key party members, which, if not controlled in the public domain, can lead to political leaders being framed negatively, and ultimately affect how they are perceived by the electorate and citizenry.

Governing Frame (Unity and Coalition)

The three newspapers were consistently uninterested in governing frames, infrequently highlighting unity and coalition talks between coalition leaders, although during this period there were various attempts at coalition between the UNC and dissident parties such as Team Unity and COP. This frame appeared an average fourteen times when coded, making it the frame least used by journalists to report on the elections. In 2001, the *Express* was most interested in unity talks, but lost interest in 2002. In contrast, *Newsday* adopted a different point of view, showing the least interest in 2001; however, that interest peaked in 2002 and then waned drastically in 2007.

The *Guardian* had the most interest in unity talks throughout the three campaign periods. In 2007, that interest reached its highest, with the increasing popularity of the COP. In 2001, unity talks were held between the NAR and Team Unity. An accommodation of sorts was also discussed between Team Unity and the PNM, although those talks were rarely reported on by the press. In 2002, unity talks were highlighted in the dailies, this time between the UNC and smaller political parties, resulting in the formation of a UNC alliance. Much excitement was created by the possibility of an alliance between the UNC alliance and COP to fight that election. However, these talks dissipated when it was perceived that unity between these two parties was not genuine and turned out to be a contrived strategy by the UNC to defeat the PNM.

Bias Scale for News Stories

An initial reading of the news stories sampled indicated there were more balanced news stories than positive or negative stories on the UNC and PNM. On average, there were close to nineteen balanced frames when compared with the number of positive and negative frames on the UNC and PNM.

During the period 2001, 2002 and 2007, the press had more positive frames on the UNC, 7.5 when compared to the the PNM's 5.8 (table 13). However, it continued to also have more negative frames on the UNC: eleven compared with the PNM's nine (table 13). On the basis of these figures, it can be concluded that the dailies tended to be balanced in their reportage of news stories; however, when they did report on the UNC, they tended to be more negative in their framing of news stories.

The same rationale holds for the comparably higher negativity towards the UNC, even though overall, the press aimed for balance and objectivity, as found in the initial reading for bias in the front pages of the three dailies.

Table 13. Bias Scale for News Stories for 2001, 2002 and 2007 Elections

Year and Newspaper	PNM		UNC		Balanced
	+	−	+	−	
2001					
Express	5	11	15	22	32
Guardian	9	7	13	13	20
Newsday	8	5	23	20	30
2002					
Express	5	10	2	9	13
Guardian	5	11	1	3	11
Newsday	8	4	2	10	12
2007					
Express	3	9	4	12	22
Guardian	5	23	7	8	16
Newsday	5	1	1	4	13
Total	53	81	68	101	169
Average	5.8	9.0	7.5	11.2	18.7

Editorials

Analysis of editorials relating to three campaign periods: 2001 (9 October–10 December), 2002 (28 August–7 October) and 2007 (28 September–5 November) in the three dailies demonstrated that editors were interested in the leadership of political parties and how they dealt with issues such as crime, corruption and leadership challenges. They were also very concerned about the role of the EBC in executing its duties in conducting fair elections. Each of the three newspapers tended to focus more on a particular leader and certain issues, but in general, whoever was the incumbent prime minister was the centre of media attention during his period in government.

Corruption

One of the main issues discussed by editors during this period was corruption by government officials, including Prime Minister Panday in 2001; the editors insisted on transparency, accountability and integrity in public office. On 17 November, in a *Guardian* editorial entitled "US$50,000 Mystery" (p. 14), the editor openly condemned the disappearance of a cheque given to Panday by party supporters for funding the UNC political campaign. The cheque was made out in Panday's name and was purportedly deposited in the UNC's account. The editor metaphorically stated that unless Panday cleared up the "mystery of the whereabouts of the US$50,000 cheque . . . the issue will remain like the legendary sword of Damocles hanging over his head" (ibid.). In a follow-up editorial entitled "Unseemly Spectacle" (30 November 2001, 16), the editor also insinuated that the police were hot on the trail in investigating the disappearance of the cheque. In 2002, in an editorial entitled "Man of Integrity" (*Newsday*, 17 November 2002, 10), reference was made to the huge sum of TT$52 million being deposited in Carlos John's personal account while he was a UNC government minister. In a follow-up editorial, "The Whole Truth" (16 September 2002, 10), the editor again raised the topic of corruption, this time mentioning the Piarco Airport project, in which contracts were awarded to friends of the UNC government without the proper tendering process being followed. *Newsday* stated that the UNC government was in denial and in a form of "self-hypnosis" about allegations of corruption, preferring to view everyone as "political enemies" with the government and stating that "it is a source of annoyance for the press to be continuously asking questions about non-existent corruption in the government" (17 November 2002, 10).

The press's continual association of Panday and his government with corrupt practices put Panday on the defensive and created very hostile and distrustful relations between the press and the government. Panday, who was not one to shy away from conflict and confrontation, described TV6, which was part of CCN, which also owned the *Express*, as the "enemy", TV6 as the "devil ... and the *Express* as the son of the devil" and called on party loyalists "to train their guns on that house" (*Express*, 24 November 2001, 10). The *Express* countered by personally attacking Panday. In an editorial entitled "Sowing the Seeds of Confusion, Anger" (6 October 2007, 12), the editor insisted that the problem within the UNC was Panday and referred to him as "a huge stumbling block" because he "refuses to give way", a man "consumed by ego" who continues "to shake the UNC Alliance to its always shaky foundation". The *Express* was even more distrustful of him, as it felt that he wanted "to win the prime minister through the back door" (11 October 2007, 12), the suggestion being that Panday was willing to manipulate the nation's constitution to stay in power. The *Express* further defended its position, insisting that its was "a sacred trust ... to help guard the society that it served from the consequences of the corrupting influences that prey on power" (24 November 2001, 10). The hostile and combative relationship between the Panday regime and the press during this period largely contributed to the public perception that the UNC government was corrupt. This negatively affected his chances of becoming prime minister again while weakening him considerably as political leader of the UNC.

Crime

A rise in crime levels was another issue addressed by editors during the campaigns; they opined that during the 2002–2007 period when Manning was prime minister, very little attention was paid to solve the escalating problem. Editors were also very concerned about his alliance with the perpetrators of the 1990 coup, the Jamaat al Muslimeen. They were very distrustful of this radical Muslim group, which had hijacked the democratically elected NAR government and held state-owned television station TTT for ransom. As watchdogs of democracy, the role of the media would have been antithetical to a forced government by a religious sect espousing Muslim doctrine.

The *Guardian* highlighted the devastating effect of crime in an editorial entitled "Deadly Threat to National Well-Being" (1 September 2002, 14), and chided Manning for being predictable for implying that there might be political motives behind kidnappings. Manning was again the target of the editorial pen in a follow-up editorial entitled "No Dismissing Crime, Mr PM" (8 September 2002, 12). The editor berated Manning for "engaging in political finger point-ing", stating that he had no one to blame but himself, as crime had risen under his watch as prime minister. In an editorial entitled "Little More Than Election Speech by Mr Manning" (*Guardian*, 14 September 2002, 14), the editor stated that Manning had doctored the statistics on crime to fool the population. The editor more or less stated that Manning was lying and referred to his state-ment as "dodgy" and a "vague political spiel" that "contained an unfortunate amount of faulty reasoning" (ibid.). During the campaign of 2007, the editor again highlighted the issue of crime and stated that the PNM was treating this serious issue as another public-relations job (*Guardian*, 21 October 2002, 28). Editors professed concern about Manning's lack of judgement and his inability to manage serious issues facing the country.

Readiness of the EBC to Hold Elections

One of the most important issues addressed over the entire campaign period was the readiness of the EBC to conduct elections. The EBC, created to con-duct free and fair elections and meant to be independent, became a matter for discussion in editorials. The rapid turnover of the four elections in seven years, from 2000 to 2007, raised the issue of the readiness of the commission to conduct elections at short notice. Editors were generally defensive of the EBC, protecting it from assaults by various governments, which in desperation to win elections as a means of retaining power tried to erode its independence, so as to have a greater influence in its elections process. Editors urged the EBC to defend its integrity by strengthening its structure, protecting its commis-sioners and striving for professionalism and non-partisanship in the conduct of its business at all times.

In a 2001 editorial entitled "Disturbing Signs from the EBC" (*Express*, 16 November 2001, 10), the editor made it apparent that he or she did not believe that the EBC was ready to hold elections and expected "an impending fiasco" to happen, as it had been verifying the voters' list while preparing for the election. The *Guardian* editor, in contrast, took a more measured approach to the EBC and described calls for the postponement of the election as an "over-reaction", stating that "the condition of the voters' list owed much to traditional disregard by voters of their obligation to notify the EBC of changes of address" (13 November 2002, 14). The *Newsday* editor had a similar view to that of the *Express*, in that he also did not believe the commission was ready for the election and suggested it had a "credibility problem" (10 November 2002, 10). The media questioned the fitness of one of the commissioners, Raoul John, to sit on the commission, stating that it was a conflict of interest, as John was also president of the Trinidad and Tobago Chamber of Industry and Commerce at that time (*Newsday*, 16 November 2002, 10).

In 2002, the editor of the *Express* had a change of opinion, moving from criticizing the EBC to calling it "a bedrock of democracy" (16 November 2002, 10), and openly defended the commission as "doing the best job it can, given the circumstances and the limitations imposed upon it by decades of government neglect" (28 September 2002, 10). The more sympathetic attitude towards the EBC by all three dailies suggested they felt that the EBC was a scapegoat for politicians who wanted to have greater influence over its election machinery to stay in power. The *Guardian* continued to be sympathetic towards the EBC even in light of deteriorating relations between the EBC and the PNM, which it felt was akin to "assault" and that the EBC was "in danger of being set up as a scapegoat" (19 September 2002, 10). In a follow-up editorial entitled "EBC timely peace move", the editor commended the EBC for "moving with the times" and called on politicians and the public to support the EBC. The *Newsday* editor was also sympathetic towards the EBC. In an editorial entitled "Dirty Challenges" (21 September 2002, 10), the editor indicated that there was a more "diabolical plan" involved than voter padding, which was to challenge the registration of voters in marginal constituencies, calling the challengers "unscrupulous people and corrupters . . . and enemies of our country . . . with a criminal mind". In a follow-up editorial, the editor urged the EBC to become more vocal regarding "fraudulent practices taking place in the marginal constituencies" (3 October 2002, 10), insisting that the commission could no longer keep quiet because of the "constitutional independence" it enjoyed, as it must now "accept the fact that it has lost its innocence".

In 2007, the issues of irregularities concerning the voting machinery, voter padding and queries about the voting list in the marginal constituencies all but disappeared, with the EBC being mentioned only briefly by the editors. There were no comments by the editors of either the *Express* or *Newsday* on this issue. It is not certain what caused this change in reporting: whether editorial decision or whether the EBC itself had done some work to clear up some of the accusations levelled at it. However, the *Guardian*, although implying that there were irregularities, still gave the EBC a thumbs-up, saying "that all seems to be well", and that the commission comprised "commissioners of experience and integrity". However, the editor ominously closed by stating "the nation will be watching them closely" in their central role of "preserving and enhancing our democracy", as they are expected "to perform at the highest possible standard of efficiency and fairness on election day" (3 November 2007, 26).

Commentaries

During the 2001 campaign, there was increased cynicism among columnists towards politicians, and high levels of disenchantment with the politics and the political system. An election-weary population was fast becoming frustrated with politicians who were not willing to make the changes needed to propel the society forward when elected to government. They were also frustrated with the Westminster political system, inherited from British colonialism, which continued the election of leaders in a majoritan system and perpetuated a winner-take-all situation. For newly democratic countries such as Trinidad and Tobago, constitutional reform seemed the most likely solution.

Express columnist Lloyd Best captured the mood of the country in one of his articles, stating that the country was "in a state of rebellion, whatever ostensibly the side. We're not fools; we know a slippery slope. And yet there's no simple escape" (17 November 2001, 11). Bukka Rennie wrote in the *Guardian*, "Politics in [Trinidad and Tobago] has been reduced to the ridiculous. . . . It is a total breakdown that has taken place" (5 December 2001, 5). Tony Fraser also wrote in the *Guardian* about the disappointment of the campaign, asking rhetorically, if no party emerged with a clear majority, "How are these politicians to convince the society they have the integrity and capacity to rise above their vulgar and petty selves in the national interest?" (6 December 2001, 17). Fraser lamented that none of the contending parties had any serious proposals to deal with constitutional reform and party funding. *Guardian* columnist Percy Cezair captured the mood when he said, "Unless whoever forms the new Government recognises that there must be and seeks to implement drastic changes to the entire system, it may sound alarming, the system may be heading toward destabilisation" (11 December 2001, 19). Cezair, similarly to Fraser, insisted that unless politicians embarked on constitutional reform, the political system would remain the same.

By 2002, less than eight months after the last election in 2001, columnists had exhausted most of the serious issues to write about. They continued to mull over campaign rhetoric in the absence of any serious discussions, reflecting the overall despondent mood of the country and citizens' weariness of elections and politicians on the whole. After three elections over the course of three years (2000, 2001, 2002), at a rate of one election per year, and with campaign periods stretching indefinitely, undue stress was placed on columnists to find new stories to write about, added to which, their increased cynicism and disillusionment with politicians and the political system made it difficult to write anything meaningful.

However, in 2007, the PNM had successfully run its full five-year term in office, and the mood of the country had become more optimistic with the emergence of a third party and talks of unity and accommodation. In addition, the COP's political leader, Winston Dookeran, excited the population with his talk of "new politics" and the possibility of a changed political system away from traditional voting patterns, based on race.

Governance by Political Leaders

The commentaries of all three newspapers reflected the growing disenchantment with the Panday government and a general distrust of politicians, which were displayed in the highly critical language used to describe the political leader of the UNC and prime minister at that time. Political pundits such as Lloyd Best, writing about Panday, stated: "Maximum leadership has been exposed in all its omnipotent importance and, irrespective of their sides, all and sundry see through it" (*Express*, 24 November 2001, 11). Best continued, "The moment Panday came to office; it was like an entire constituency of smart-men saw opportunity." *Express* columnist Lennox Grant described Panday "as a campaigner-orator, performer, and stand-up comic, and ever-calculating manipulator" (17 November 2001, 11). Selwyn Ryan in the *Express* stated that Panday "has been a dismal failure . . . he found it difficult to make the transition from political pugilist to statesman" (18 November 2001, 13), and that his regime was associated with corruption and state plunder. Columnist Suzanne Mills wrote in *Newsday*, "There is strong anti-Hindu, Panday, UNC and EBC sentiment in the country accompanied by awful undertones of 'All Indians thief and they going to steal the election'." Mills further wrote about "lack of trust . . . and echoes of animosity" towards Panday by the general population (18 November 2001, 10).

Manning also attracted media attention because of his highly unpopular decisions, which did not augur well for the population, such as aligning with the perpetrators of the 1990 coup, the Jamaat al Muslimeen, and his decision to hire friends and family for key ministerial positions in his cabinet. *Express* columnist Raoul Pantin stated that Manning had made "a colossal blunder" and that he was leading the country down a similar path to Jamaica, where politicians allegedly linked with known criminals to win elections (15 September 2002, 11). Similarly, Raffique Shah also questioned Manning's tactics, announcing that he was "digging his own political grave" (15 September 2002, 11), by collaborating with the Muslimeen. However, although they felt that Manning had made a serious blunder, the media also felt that Panday was exploiting Manning's lapse in judgement by insinuating that the country's democracy, led by the PNM, would be heavily influenced by this radical Muslim group. The nation of Trinidad and Tobago has always prided itself on being a mosaic of cultures, in which all ethnicities have the freedom to practise their religions. The fear that one radical Muslim group could infringe on that freedom by heavily influencing national policies, together with the memory of the 1990 coup, disturbed the non-Muslim segments of the population, especially the large Hindu community that generally formed the base of the UNC party. Ryan succinctly stated that Panday was using the information "to terrorize the population especially Indians and middle class persons" (15 September 2002, 11) to distract from accusations of corruption.

Race

Most columnists in all three newspapers continued to show considerable maturity in their discussions on race, preferring to caution leaders to desist from appealing to race during the campaign. Although columnists were generally critical of Panday's leadership, they openly credited him for his inclusionist policy, which was more attractive to non-Indians compared with that of the PNM, although they felt he used the race card to his advantage. Selwyn Ryan commended Panday for ethnic and class inclusion, saying he must be "given credit for helping the society to manage a soft landing on the ethnic issue in December 1995" (*Express*, 18 November 2001, 13). Columnist Indira Maharaj also credited Panday for the multiracial composition of the UNC party and for ushering a new era of politics of accommodation and inclusion.

There were some strong pro-UNC views among certain columnists who regarded race as the determining factor in certain national policies of the PNM. For example, *Express* columnist Indira Maharaj accused the PNM of having a racial cultural policy when she argued that the "peripheralization of Indian culture and authentic African culture was the order of the day" (16 November 2001, 11). This, she said, was reflected in the imbalance of Indian recipients of national awards. Columnist Sat Maharaj similarly accused the PNM of using education to exploit children and to perpetuate "cultural and social engineering" (15 September 2002, 11) not for nation-building purposes but, from his point of view, to service a more sinister objective. Similarly, Anand Ramlogan, writing in 2001, alluded to race's being a main factor in the PNM's cultural policy that he felt marginalized and alienated the Indian population while deliberatively stifling Indian culture. He also accused the PNM of discriminating against Indian politicians in the cabinet (*Guardian*, 7 September 2002, 15). Ramlogan was a lawyer who had built a reputation fighting for people who were denied promotions in the public service because of political victimization. Ramlogan was expressing views shared by certain elements within the East Indian community who felt that the PNM was deliberately alienating East Indians through racist national policies to maintain political power. It also showed the deep distrust that existed between the two largest ethnic groups on matters related to race, culture, political power relations and economic distribution.

Express columnist Raffique Shah lamented that even though political leaders had tried to bridge the gap between the races, Trinidadians continued to be identified by their ethnicity, so that Indians were automatically assumed to be UNC and Africans to be PNM (1 November 2002, 12). Shah warned that if nationals did not check themselves, the country could be torn apart. However, although the latent racial feelings among the East Indian segment of the population were managed by newspapers, at the same time, they allowed ample space for the airing of these views without making them the most dominant theme in the election.

Gender as a Main Factor in the Election

For the first time in the history of Trinidad and Tobago's politics, gender became a major factor in an internal party election when Kamla Persad-Bissessar emerged as the first woman within the UNC to contest the post of party leader. The nation's politics were mostly male-dominated, with the UNC typically viewed as a man's club. Many felt that Persad-Bissessar's place in politics was achieved as a result of the patronage of her mentor and political leader, Basdeo Panday. On several occasions, Persad-Bissessar proved her loyalty to her political leader by stepping aside on his request; for instance, after a short period as attorney general, she stepped aside to make way for Ramesh Lawrence Maharaj to replace her. Many felt that Persad-Bissessar, an accomplished lawyer in her own right, was deserving of the position and was simply being sidelined by transfer to the Ministry of Education because of her gender. Persad-Bissessar did not protest. However, when history proved unkind to her a second time and she was publicly sidelined for the position of political leader of the UNC by Panday, she received tremendous support from various columnists in all three dailies. Columnists reflected the general feeling on the ground that Persad-Bissessar was deserving of the position, and some even expressed the view that she was a strong contender for prime minister of the country. Persad-Bissessar's attempts to ascend to the highest office in her party found sympathy with women who were facing similar challenges in their workplace or at home, where some might have felt oppressed. Women in Trinidad and Tobago had surpassed men in education, and many had reached top positions in their jobs; however, chief executive officer positions were still dominated by men, and the boardrooms by and large remained a male domain. These factors may well have been working subliminally in the national consciousness of women in Trinidad and Tobago and manifested in a yearning for the right female to ascend to the highest political office at a time when frustration with male political leaders had heightened. These sentiments together with the challenges faced by Persad-Bissessar may have flowed into an emerging current and helped strengthen it. *Guardian* columnist Dana Seetahal wrote, "It seems to me that the UNC is not only a Panday fiefdom, but it is one where women are expected to perform a subsidiary role, as in the women's contingent, not really at one with the big boys" (14 October 2007, 35).

Similarly, *Express* columnist Bunny Rambhajan wrote of Persad-Bissessar's inability as a woman to be taken seriously within the party: "Panday may have seen Persad-Bissessar as a protégée, maybe even as a daughter, and her competence and ability are obvious. But I suspect that he has never seen her, and will never see her as a real peer, or an equal. After all she is just a woman" (7 October 2007, 12). Suzanne Sheppard in *Newsday* stated that "Kamla, more than any other woman in TT's recent political history, has come close to shattering the glass ceiling more than once, only to be shunted aside" (14 October 2007, 12).

Although most columnists bestowed praises on Persad-Bissessar for the dignified way in which she handled her public humiliation, there was a sense of frustration with her in that she continued to play the role of subservient follower and bow to the whims of the party leader. Raffique Shah wrote: "Never before, though, have I witnessed a woman shafted by two men at the same time in front of 40,000 people . . . and take it with a smile. . . . Amazing, I tell you. She swallowed pride, prejudice, and womanhood, all in a few gulps" (*Express*, 14 October 2007, 12).

The issue of gender, based on the rising popularity of Persad-Bissessar, had begun to take form in 2007 and came to full fruition by the time of the 2010 election, from which she emerged as prime minister.

Coalition/Unity Talks between the UNC Alliance and COP

Political parties in Trinidad and Tobago were generally inclined to hold unity/coalition talks with either dissenting or opposing parties, especially when they felt that that party could enhance their chances of capturing the government. The emergence of new formations in the political arena, especially when they seemed genuine and could effect change in the political system, brought new hope to the citizenry, which was reflected in the sentiments expressed by certain columnists. However, given the 1986 NAR experience, columnists were much more sceptical about the way coalitions were being hastily put together. The year when the COP was formed was no exception. According to *Guardian* columnist John La Guerre, this was partly because of the manner in which these talks were conducted, with Panday extending an invitation to the COP leader, Winston Dookeran, on the one hand while referring to his party as a "corpse" on the other hand (30 September 2007, 21). Panday's coleader, Jack

Warner, worsened the situation by trying to force unity talks between the two parties, which columnist and renowned lawyer Dana Seetahal described as "attempted intimidation" (ibid., 31). Seetahal further stated that Panday was the greatest hindrance to unity, and his efforts hypocritical, as "he had emasculated the titular leader in front of the whole world". Seetahal was referring to Dookeran's being forced out of the UNC, after he was elected political leader, by Panday, who refused to relinquish the position to him. For Dookeran to accept an invitation from Panday, Seetahal wrote, would be tantamount to "political suicide".

Selwyn Ryan and Hamid Ghany opined that should Dookeran accept Panday's invitation to join the UNC, there would be "massive haemorrhaging from the COP" (*Express*, 28 October 2007, 11), and Dookeran would lose "any credibility as a serious political leader in the society" (*Guardian*, 21 October 2007, 30). Ghany further stated that part of the attractiveness of the COP "is based on the venom that the UNC leadership has poured over Winston Dookeran", and that he would lose a large portion of the UNC heartland should he join with the UNC alliance.

Winston Dookeran was viewed as "[a]n individual political leader", with a fairly clean slate going into the 2007 election. "He has no past history of pursuing personal agendas at the expense of party and nation . . . of being haunted with corruption and no tendency to savage individuals" (*Guardian*, 3 October 2007, 31). This clean image represented by the COP leader and his party was a direct contrast to that presented by the two traditional parties and their respective leaders. Columnists were afraid that the new force would be corrupted by the parent party, the UNC, thereby stymieing the development of politics in the country. As a consequence, several of the columnists were opposed to any form of coalition.

Conclusion

Analysis of all three newspapers over the course of the three campaign periods disclosed that although the three dailies achieved balance in their covers and news reports, there was a tendency for them to frame elections around political personalities, with an emphasis on the leaders of the parties. However, it was found that the UNC leader, Basdeo Panday, had more negative frames when compared with the PNM political leader, Patrick Manning, which adversely affected Panday's chances of recapturing government. Partisan bias was also displayed towards the new political party, COP, and its leader, Winston Dookeran, in 2007.

The balance achieved was most likely a result of the increased professionalism of editors within media houses, which ensured partisan and structural biases were kept in check in a situation in which newsrooms were staffed by journalists and media practitioners of diverse political orientations. The strict adherence to the editorial process, as well as self-censorship mechanisms put in place by the media (for example, media codes of ethics) ensured that biases were reined in early in the editing process.

The tendency to be more negative towards the UNC while focusing mostly on its political leader, Panday, was directly related to allegations of corruption, in-party fighting among the UNC executive members and scandals that were prevalent during the UNC regime and that remained with it when it left office. Journalists reported the news as it unfolded daily, without offering opinions. Both negative and positive stories were given prominence on front pages on the basis of their currency and newsworthiness. However, evidence points to editorial and reporters' biases in the selection of news items, which determined the daily agenda of the newspapers, as there was a tendency to select headlines and news items related to corruption and conflict in the UNC, which reflected negatively on the Panday regime.

A similar trend was discerned with regard to the PNM, with all three newspapers becoming increasingly negative towards the PNM from 2001 to 2007, whereas earlier they were consistently negative towards the UNC. However, the number of negative headlines about the UNC was more than those about the PNM. Editors of the three dailies generally reported events as they unfolded each day, and as both parties had their fair share of scandals and conflicts, they were reported on as they occurred. The increasingly negative headlines attributed to the PNM suggested that whichever government was in office was most likely to be held up for public scrutiny by the press, which is best described as the "negative incumbency effect".

In terms of frames, politician-as-a-personality was the most popular frame used, with politicians other than the two political leaders being highly framed by journalists. The focus on personality frame indicated that the press was concerned about the leadership of the country and in ensuring that the right person was chosen as prime minister. Over the course of the seven years under review, two other leaders emerged from the formation of new political parties – Ramesh Maharaj of Team Unity in 2001 and Winston Dookeran of the COP in 2007 – but both were rejected by the population. Regarding the COP leader, evidence pointed to partisan bias towards that party; however, even though he received considerable support from the press, he was unsuccessful in winning over enough of the population to win a seat in parliament. In this situation, the press was unable to influence the outcome of the 2007 election, even though Dookeran was portrayed as the most suitable candidate to win and lead the country.

The issue frame was the second most popular frame used by journalists. However, when compared with the politician-as-a-personality frame, this frame was used moderately, reaching an all-time low in 2007. Issues were discussed infrequently during the campaigns, and in general, journalists reported what was discussed by politicians on political platforms. The other frames (horse-race, conflict and governing) were used even less frequently over the course of the three years, with *Newsday* mostly focusing on horse-race frames, and the *Express* on conflicts. The *Guardian* was more concerned with the governing frame, defined as unity talks that held the possibility of leading to a coalition.

Editorials

The dominant issues that engaged editorial attention and became two of the main agenda items during the campaigns were corruption as it related to political office held by the Panday government and fear of corrupting political influences on the fairness of the independent election authority, the EBC. Governance issues such as managing high crime levels and political affiliations with criminal elements in the society were also of major concern to editors.

Regarding corruption, evidence pointed to editors, especially those in the *Express*, using more frames on corruption when writing about the Panday government, which inadvertently influenced public perception that the UNC party and government were corrupt. Panday's vociferous and consistent defence of his government and his insistence that his party had done no wrong worsened the situation and resulted in even more strained relations between him and the media, especially the *Express*. The fact that during the three election periods Panday adopted a very confrontational and combative stance towards the media largely contributed to the hostility directed at him by the press and alienated him from the media. In addition, the chief executive officer of the *Express*, Ken Gordon, was involved in a bitter court battle against Panday in which Gordon accused Panday of calling him a pseudo-racist. Under such circumstances, relations between the *Express* and Panday worsened, affecting the slant and tone of the *Express* editorials, which tended to veer towards the negative, as shown in their less-than-flattering assessment of Panday's character, their distrust of his motives in picking Jack Warner as the UNC leader over Persad-Bissessar and strong condemnation of his handling of the gender issue in his party. One can conclude, on the basis of the evidence presented here, that the *Express* exhibited structural bias against Panday in its editorials during these three elections.

However, editors were also unforgiving of Manning's flippant attitude to serious issues that affected the nation, such as crime, his links with the Jamaat al Muslimeen and his tendency to politicize state institutions such as the EBC. Their selection of these issues framed Manning as a political animal who would do anything to retain power – someone with misplaced priorities and questionable judgement. Although the editors of the three dailies shared similar views, they tended to have views of different strengths regarding particular issues and personalities; for example, the *Express* focused highly on Panday, corruption and conflicts, whereas the *Guardian* mostly turned its attention towards governance issues and Manning.

Columns

All three newspapers continued to treat the issues of leadership, race, governance, and unity and coalition talks in a fashion similar to the editorials. In general, whichever political leader was in the seat of government, that leader was under scrutiny by the press, as seen with Panday in 2001 and 2002 and Manning in 2007. The press insisted on its "watchdog" role, holding leaders accountable to the electorate and ensuring the smooth functioning of the election system, devoid of political interference with the conduct of free and fair elections.

Columnists also focused highly on the UNC government and its political leader, Basdeo Panday. Some columnists declared their support for the PNM or the UNC. However, the views of these select columnists did not appear to reflect the views of the editors of newspapers, with ample space reserved for people of diverse political orientations to air their views. During the 2007 campaign, the press allocated equal space to political parties, with both the UNC and COP having regular columns to present their positions.

Regarding the issue of race, the press consistently showed maturity by downplaying an issue that threatened to polarize the society if not handled carefully. Race had always been part of the reality of Trinidad and Tobago's politics, with the two largest ethnic groups – East Indians and Africans – forming the backbone of the two leading political parties. Editors generally distanced themselves from the views of certain columnists who had strong opinions on race and made no attempt to sensationalize the issue or make it into a national issue, which could have become very divisive and disruptive with regard to the politics of the country. It was a period in which racial profiling of political parties had started blurring, with the UNC, previously seen as a stereotypical East Indian party, being viewed as more inclusive, especially with Jack Warner as a frontline member and coleader together with its founder, Basdeo Panday. The COP followers were mostly diverse and included supporters from both traditional parties. Although columnists were partisan to the COP as a party, they were disapproving of superficial attempts at alliances and unity between the COP and the UNC.

Also for the first time in the history of Trinidad and Tobago's politics, gender became a force to be reckoned with, with Persad-Bissessar being framed as a woman striving for gender equality in a male-dominated world of party politics. At the same time, the UNC was framed as a clique of traditional East Indian men who viewed women as incapable of holding high positions and better relegated to supporting roles in the party. Persad-Bissessar was also framed as a person with the potential to become more than a party leader if given the opportunity. She emerged at a time when women had begun to have a serious effect on politics globally, including Hillary Clinton, who vied for the presidential seat in the highly publicized 2008 election in the United States. Other Indian subcontinental female leaders had also emerged in its male-dominated society, such as Sonia Gandhi in India (who, however, had to cede the prime ministership to a man, although she wielded the most power in the party) and Benazir Bhutto in Pakistan, who emerged as a barrier-breaker in a male-dominated society before her untimely violent death.

It is clear that 2001, 2002 and 2007, as election years between the return to power of the UNC in 2000 (after the second defeat of the PNM in 1995) and the emergence of the UNC-led coalition PP in 2010, were transition years in the political life of Trinidad and Tobago. The media as a mediating force between the views of politicians and the feelings and aspirations of the population seemed to be reflecting this in both their coverage of the elections and their editorial analysis. There was scepticism of both leaders of the major, traditional political parties and their leadership. New leaders were emerging, corruption was a dominant concern both at the political and institutional level and the gender factor, as well as the succession factor, had emerged.

CHAPTER 6

Case Analysis of the 2010 Election in Trinidad and Tobago

THE YEAR 2010 WAS A HISTORIC ONE FOR politics in Trinidad and Tobago, as the country welcomed a new coalition government led by a female prime minister, successfully breaking the monopoly on national politics held by the UNC and the PNM. It was also a period of major changes in party politics, as the two leaders, Patrick Manning and Basdeo Panday, were faced with leadership challenges within their own political parties. For the UNC, the role and structure of the party was changed considerably when Kamla Persad-Bissessar emerged as political leader of the party, replacing its founding leader, Basdeo Panday. She was also successful in bringing together a coalition of opposition parties: the COP, the Movement for Social Justice, the National Joint Action Committee and the TOP, to fight the 2010 election under the umbrella of the PP.

It was a time when sweeping political changes were occurring worldwide: The first black American had emerged as the president of the United States on 4 November 2008, and the UK election (6 May 2010), coming three weeks before Trinidad and Tobago's election on 24 May 2010, resulted in a hung parliament, with the government eventually being formed by a coalition led by Conservative leader David Cameron. These two landmark events, which changed politics in two of the most influential countries in the world, made changes in local politics seem even more possible. Trinidadians frustrated with the deadlock held by the two traditional parties, the UNC and PNM, were also anxious to welcome changes in national politics, especially in the context of sweeping changes also taking place regionally. It was also a period in which many strong female prime ministers and presidents had emerged internationally, including

Angela Merkel in Germany (2005), Yulia Tymoshenko of Ukraine (2005) and Benazir Bhutto of Pakistan (1988, 1993). Closer to home, in Latin America and the Caribbean, several women had ascended to the highest political office in their countries: Portia Simpson-Miller in Jamaica (2006), Michelle Bachelet in Chile (2006) and Cristina Fernández de Kirchner of Argentina (2007). The stage seemed set for the first female prime minister also to emerge in Trinidad and Tobago.

At the time of the campaign, the PNM was in its second term of government, but called an election in midterm, long before the due date, for 24 May 2010. By that time, however, the government, led by Prime Minister Manning, had become very unpopular because of the leadership style of Manning and disapproval of his government's policy decisions, with their focus on large building projects, which many felt was a waste of the country's resources, derived from the rise in the price of oil. The scandals and corruption arising from the award of building contracts and procurement practices, together with the government's attack on the press for biased reporting, further worsened relations between the state and the media. Manning's public fight with his former deputy political leader Keith Rowley had a bruising effect on the prime minister within his own party, and the government's inability to solve the escalating crime problem, together with the prime minister's perceived arrogance, further alienated him from the population.

Front Pages

All three newspapers focused heavily on the election on their front pages and in news stories during the forty-five days of campaigning. However, the *Guardian* had the most extensive coverage during the period, with approximately 98 per cent of its front pages dedicated to the election. It was followed by the *Express,* with 91.11 per cent and *Newsday* at 84.44 per cent (table 14). The figures indicated that all three newspapers, especially the *Guardian,* focused heavily on the general election, and that the 2010 national election was a highly publicized event, with electoral coverage being given national prominence over all other issues taking place. The percentage of coverage on front pages during the 2010 election campaign, compared with the coverage in the preceding elections throughout the decade, is noteworthy and may reflect a higher level of interest in the 2010 election for a number of reasons.

Table 14. Number of Front Pages on 2010 Election

Newspapers	Number of Front Pages	%
Guardian	44	97.78
Express	41	91.11
Newsday	38	84.44
Total	123	273.33
Average	41	91.11

The heavy coverage of this election was mainly due to convulsions taking place on the political landscape; namely, the rising popularity of an opposition leader who was also a woman and the fact that she was leading a coalition of parties against the PNM. That coalition, which presented itself as the PP, consisted of five political parties: the UNC, COP, TOP, Movement for Social Justice and National Joint Action Committee.

The coalition movement was rapidly garnering support from the population and seemed poised to defeat the PNM at the polls. In addition, the UNC campaign was managed by an international consultant who had been part of President Obama's presidential campaign team in 2008, and the possibility of similar results occurring in Trinidad made this a high-interest election keenly followed by all those who were looking on, including the media. The *Guardian* also had its own election "war room", which tracked the campaign daily in this particular election.

Photos

All three newspapers focused on group photos rather than feature either the UNC or PNM political leader alone on their front covers (table 15). The main reason was that the coalition movement, the PP, involved a number of political leaders and personalities who were also given ample coverage on the covers such as the National Joint Action Committee's Makandal Daaga; the TOP's Ashworth Jack; the COP's Winston Dookeran; and the Movement for Social Justice's Errol McLeod. In addition, because of the challenges and conflicts within the PNM hierarchy, several of the party stalwarts such as Keith Rowley and Ken Valley were also placed on the covers at varying times.

Table 15. Number of Photos of Politicians on Front Pages for 2010 Election

News papers	Opposition Leader*	Opposition Leader Alone	Prime Minister†	Prime Minister Alone	Both	Other Politicians
Guardian	17	10	12	5	6	28
Express	9	2	10	4	6	20
Newsday	15	8	9	3	6	16
Total	41	20	31	12	18	64

*Kamla Persad-Bissessar

†Patrick Manning.

However, when they did feature the political leader of the PP and the PNM, they were more often featured together rather than alone. When featured alone, the opposition leader, Persad-Bissessar, appeared more times alone than the prime minister (20:12) on the front pages of both the *Guardian* (10:5) and *Newsday* (8:3) (table 15).

Persad-Bissessar was frequently featured because of the consistent manoeuvrings and brokering of deals between the UNC and the various other parties as the coalition movement took shape, and these were generally prioritized by editors as the daily news to be featured on the covers. In addition, she had become a political celebrity and was featured prominently on the covers. This is in direct contrast to previous elections, in which the incumbent prime minister was, as a rule, featured more than the opposition leader.

Conversely, the *Express* featured the prime minister more often than the opposition leader. Manning was featured twice as much as the UNC leader (4:2), although in most instances the photos of Manning were not positive. In contrast, the photos of the UNC political leader appeared smiling and happy; those of Manning looked troubled and disturbed.

Headlines

All three newspapers carried a more balanced number of headlines on the front pages (UNC, 35; PNM, 32), indicating that editors did strive for objectivity in determining the daily news agenda. There was a greater propensity to be

Table 16. Bias Scale of Headlines on Front Pages for 2010 Election

Newspaper	UNC			PNM		
	+	–	B	+	–	B
Newsday	11	0	11	4	16	9
Guardian	9	5	15	3	15	15
Express	8	4	9	7	17	8
Total	28	9	35	14	48	32

negative to the PNM than the UNC (UNC, 9; PNM, 48), *Newsday* carrying no negative headlines on the UNC at all (UNC, 0; PNM, 16) (table 16). This negativity surrounding the PNM was directly related to conflicts among the key figures in the party, as well as allegations of scandals and corruption that surrounded the PNM's term in office.

In contrast, the three newspapers were twice as often positive to the UNC as the PNM (UNC, 28; PNM, 14), mainly as a result of the tremendous goodwill the PP had mustered from the media as well as the fact that the PP was not in government and therefore had no record of policy decisions and/or track record to defend.

The PP also made news because it was involved in unity and coalition talks, which were generally viewed as positive for the country's healthy democracy and for fostering a cross-ethnic spirit of unity. In addition, Persad-Bissessar received tremendous goodwill from the media during the internal fight for the leadership of the UNC because she conducted a clean campaign. This, together, with her affable personality, made her a much-liked person. The press was also sympathetic towards her because of the savagery of the personal attacks made against her by her own colleagues in the UNC, who sought to discredit her leadership capabilities and publicly humiliate her. She was also viewed as a novelty because she was the first woman to lead a local political party, all of which made good news and sold newspapers.

Analysis of News Stories

During the forty-five days of campaigning, 167 political news stories were ana-lysed, of which 50 were from *Newsday*, 55 from the *Express* and 67 from the

Guardian (table 17). The most dominant frame was politician-as-a-personality, with other politicians also being profiled alongside both the prime minister and political leader of the PP. This is in keeping with trends found in previous elections, in which the prime minister was the centre of media attention.

As found in previous elections, the incumbent prime minister was at the forefront of news reporting inside the newspapers. Similarly, the prime minister was considered the main source of government information, and as he was the person entrusted with governing the country, his every movement was followed by the press. In addition, he had in his employ a host of professional communications personnel, such as public-relations and communications specialists, who ensured that he was in the media daily.

The horse-race frame was the second most popular frame used during the campaign, and although this was somewhat different from previous elections, the fiercely fought race to the polls between the governing PNM and the coalition movement became a much anticipated and reported event in newspapers. This contest, which was fought in the public domain, became highly mediatized, with the population looking on ringside. The media also played a mediating role during the ensuing battle, ensuring that both sides were well represented on their pages, even going as far as calling for national debates between the two political leaders, as is generally the practice in democratic elections in the United States and United Kingdom. As a result, issues were pushed to the background and conflict and governing frames were pushed down in priority by the press. One may argue that inherent in the call for debates was a demand for discussion of issues, but one cannot deny that debates also focused on personalities and on contest and competition; that is, the horse-race aspect of the election. In terms of governing frame, the PP was less concerned, in campaign

Table 17. Frames of News Stories for 2010 Election

Newspaper	Number of Articles	Issue Frame	Politician (Kamla)	Politician (Manning)	Politician (Other)	Governing (Unity, Coalitions)	Conflict	Horse R (Opinic Polls)
Newsday	50	219	117	251	544	163	229	47(
Express	55	310	180	249	251	75	37	14₄
Guardian	67	336	225	365	413	87	125	33₆
Total	167	865	522	865	1,208	325	391	92(
Average	55.67	288.33	174.00	288.33	402.67	108.33	130.33	306.6:

Table 18. Bias Scale for News Stories for 2010 Election

Newspaper	UNC Coalition/Peoples Partnership			PNM		
	+	−	B	+	−	B
Newsday	2	2	8	1	13	7
Express	5	2	19	7	11	18
Guardian	7	5	23	5	17	22
Total	14	9	50	13	41	47

mode, about how to govern, and instead focused its efforts on – as might be expected – putting the architecture of the partnership together and building a united force strong enough to defeat the incumbent PNM government.

Yet the press did not focus on or stress the governance issues in the context of an emerging predetermined coalition of parties in the election.

In general, journalists strove for balance in framing news stories, with little difference between the PP and PNM. Likewise, they tended to be equally positive to both parties. However, an initial reading of the news stories disclosed a strong propensity to be negative to the PNM when compared with coverage of the PP.

Personality Frame

The two leading personalities who were framed during the 2010 election were Persad-Bissessar and Manning. During the 2010 election, the opposition leader, Persad-Bissessar, as the first female contender for prime minister of the country, used her ability to bring together several opposition parties under the umbrella of unity and gained tremendous mass support, popularly described as "Kamlamania". The momentum gathered force when the possibility of defeating the PNM and forming the next government seemed real. The press, wanting to capture the mood of the country while providing the population with timely information on the opposition leader, documented her every move in newsprint, catapulting her to celebrity status.

The PNM's political leader and prime minister of the country also became the centre of attention of the media and was featured more times in their news stories inside the newspapers than the UNC's political leader. In most instances, this coverage tended to be more negative towards Manning and was referred to as the "Manning factor" by columnist Selwyn Ryan (16 May 2010, 13). The Manning factor grew in momentum as coverage in the press became more negative, and he became associated with hubris and all the negativity associated with his government, such as the scandals, corruption and conflicts. Although media attention worked positively for the UNC's political leader, it tended to have a negative effect on the PNM's leader, causing him to lose popularity. According to Selwyn Ryan, *Express* political columnist, "My own field work shows that the Manning factor is that which impacts negatively on the PNM's campaign" (16 May 2010, 13). What could possibly be interpreted as media bias in the way the press covered Manning may well have been a society reaching a point at which the people had turned against their leader, simultaneously feeling the need to find someone else to embrace in the spirit of hope. In each election, the challenge has always been finding the right leader to lead the country.

One can conclude that the change in government was influenced somewhat by the declining popularity of political leaders on the one hand and the simultaneously increasing popularity of the opposition leader on the other, resulting in the opposition leader's being given equal or more coverage than the prime minister. Therefore, negative coverage of a leader in the press could position that leader for a fall by influencing how voters think about that person and how they act during elections. At the same time, the way the press frames opposition leaders could affect their fortunes at the polls.

Elections as a Horse-Race Frame

Both *Newsday* and the *Guardian* focused most of their reporting on the two main political parties, the PNM and the UNC, and the contest for the prize of winning the general election and the right to govern the country. They also focused on the contest for leadership of both political parties, such as whether Persad-Bissessar was the most suitable person to lead the partnership and the country compared with Winston Dookeran, Makandal Daaga, Errol McLeod and Ashworth Jack. In the PNM, media attention focused on the contest between Manning and rivals Keith Rowley and Pennelope Beckles, both of whom were highly popular among PNM supporters and were a main challenge for leadership of the PNM party.

The media also published political polls conducted during the period by independent pollsters such as the North American Caribbean Teachers Association and the ANSA McAL Psychological Research Centre at the University of the West Indies, which focused on issues such as leadership of parties and country, preferred choices of constituents and likely winner of the elections. Several polls were undertaken by both local and foreign pollsters that helped position Persad-Bissessar as the most attractive candidate to lead the country and become prime minister, thanks to the results that were emerging. A North American Caribbean Teachers Association poll in April 2010 stated that 70 per cent of people polled indicated Persad-Bissessar should be the leader of any accommodation forged between the UNC and the COP, over Winston Dookeran (24 per cent) (*Express*, 14 April 2010, 29). The poll also stated that Persad-Bissessar was more liked than the current prime minister, Patrick Manning, with a favourability rating of 51 per cent against Manning's 31 per cent and Dookeran's 26 per cent (*Express*, 24 April 2010, 17). An ANSA McAL poll published in the *Trinidad Guardian* (16 May 2010, A12) indicated that 47 per cent of the population was most likely to vote for the UNC coalition against the PNM (25 per cent), with 55 per cent believing Persad-Bissessar was the most suitable person to lead the country compared with Manning's and Dookeran's 1 per cent.

During a tight race to the finish line, independent pollsters may be used by the press to influence the way the public thinks about candidates for elections. Clearly, the press was trying to influence how the citizenry perceived Persad-Bissessar and may have influenced how they acted on election day, although other factors were also at play here.

Conflict Frame

Conflicts within the parties and between the two political parties were only moderately reported on by the three newspapers, with *Newsday* focusing the most on conflicts (229 stories) (table 17) compared with the *Express* (37 stories) and the *Guardian* (125 stories) (table 17). Conflicts were not considered a central issue in the 2010 election, with the media generally shying away from internal fighting within the PP and the PNM. The media focused more on conflicts within the PNM, in terms of the infighting between the PNM political leader and his deputy Keith Rowley (*Guardian*, 15 April 2010, A5; *Newsday*, 28 April 2010, 3). *Newsday* also highlighted the conflict between Manning and

Pennelope Beckles (*Newsday*, 16 April 2010, 17, 3), a potential challenger for the leadership of the party.

There were even fewer reports on conflicts within the UNC. Early in the campaign, there appeared to be hints of conflict between the new UNC leader, Kamla Persad-Bissessar, and former leader Basdeo Panday over the sidelining of his daughter Mickela Panday as a candidate for the general election (*Express*, 1 May 2010, 17). Conflicts also occurred between the political leader and Panday loyalists such as Vasant Bharath Kelvin Ramnath, Hamza Rafeeq and Ramesh Maharaj (*Newsday*, 26 April and 1 May 2010, 3). However, the press handled these conflicts sensitively and did not sensationalize what could easily have escalated into more explosive situations.

Issue Frames

The reporting of meaningful issues that affected the overall governance of the country was not given extensive media coverage and was generally secondary to electoral coverage of political personalities. The *Guardian* reported most on national issues, indicating that the newspaper had deep interest in the development of the country. However, the issue frame was the one used second most frequently by the *Express*, indicating that both newspapers placed some emphasis on developmental issues that affected the population. Issues that were highly reported on and were generally the focus of much of the election were corruption and scandal, as well as media bias. Other issues, such as abuse of power by the state, the independence of the judiciary, the provision of social services and education, were mentioned with limited media exploration.

Corruption and Scandal Issues

Corruption and scandals surrounding the PNM government were major issues during the 2010 election. The biggest scandal concerned the state-owned Urban Development Corporation of Trinidad and Tobago (UDeCOTT), which was responsible for large projects worth millions of dollars. The high-handedness, lack of transparency and lack of accountability of this state entity to the minister of trade and industry, Keith Rowley, led to a major brawl between the minister and UDeCOTT's chairman, Calder Hart, resulting in the prime minister unceremoniously and publicly firing Rowley as a cabinet minister for "washing the PNM's dirty linen in public" (*Newsday*, 18 April 2010, 10). (Rowley had been the line minister responsible for UDeCOTT when he was minister of planning and development, prior to becoming minister of trade and industry.) This was followed by the scandal surrounding the extremely close relationship between the prime minister and Calder Hart, as well as allegations of close links between Hart's wife and a Malaysian company used by UDeCOTT to supply workers for building projects in Trinidad and Tobago.

Another scandal that gripped the media was the close relationship between Manning and his spiritual adviser, Juliana Pena, and state funds originally meant for an extension of the prime minister's residence being secretly used to construct a church on state land in the Heights of Guanapo for his spiritual adviser (*Express*, 16 May 2010, 3). Another scandal that riveted the populace was the sudden increased wealth of one of Manning's ministers – it was alleged that he had acquired an expensive house in one of the most exclusive residential areas, even though it would have been difficult to afford such an investment as a salaried government minister. This situation worsened when it was disclosed that he was still an ordained Catholic priest, and married, while acting as a government minister.

Governance: Coalition Frame

Coalition frame was the least prominent frame used by journalists to report news stories in all three newspapers, even though several dissident groups and opposition forces came together to form an opposition party to contest the general election. Originally, media attention focused on coalition talks between the UNC and COP to contest the 2010 election. However, media hype intensified when other forces representing Tobago, the trade unions, the Black Power Movement and other activist groups came together with the more dominant UNC to contest the election under the umbrella of the PP (*Guardian*, 10 April 2010, 3). But not all reporting on unity talks was positive. The PNM leader tried to instil fear in the minds of the citizenry about the uncertainty of having a coalition government, which he said had a history of failure (*Guardian*, 18 March 2010, 3). He cited the UNC's track record on governance, which he said was a failure compared with the stability of the PNM government (*Newsday*, 24 April 2010, 3). Beyond this, the media news stories generally paid little attention to governance issues, such as what might happen after the coalition won the election, who would become president, how portfolios would be shared, what would be its plan of action, how it would govern, what could happen if the coalition should fall apart and so forth. Although both parties did develop manifestoes, these were not reported on extensively.

Editorials

All three newspapers addressed similar issues in their editorials. These included governance issues such as crime and integrity in office, corruption and media bias. They were also very concerned about the coalition movement headed by the UNC leader, Kamla Persad-Bissessar.

Governance under Prime Minister Patrick Manning

Throughout the 2010 campaign, Manning continued to lose the favour of the newspapers' editors because of his style of governance and the way he handled leadership challenges and conflict within his own party. The prime minister's attack on the media, accusing them of biased reporting against his government, only worsened relations between the press and politicians, making it even more difficult for the dailies to do their jobs as a free press with objectivity and independence. Editors of all three dailies were highly incensed over the prime minister's unwillingness to reveal the date of the election, his reluctance to participate in a live televised debate with the opposition leader, his use of race on the political platform and his public fight with his former deputy political leader Keith Rowley.

In an effort to lift the national discourse, and following in the footsteps of live debates between presidential and prime-ministerial candidates in the US and UK elections, similar televised debates were being encouraged by the business sector in Trinidad and Tobago, which had formed a National Debates Commission. Editors became highly incensed when Manning refused to participate in these debates, with one editorial encouraging him to "step up to the podium" (*Express*, 29 April 2010, 3), and insisting that he should have leapt at "the opportunity to demolish the alleged weakling", Persad-Bissessar, to whom Manning had referred previously in a derogatory manner. The editor insisted that by not agreeing to the debate, Manning had made "the most nakedly political admission", insinuating that Manning considered himself superior to everyone, including the opposition leader, whom he branded "a weakling". The editor indicated that a debate would give Manning a "different face" in terms of "character, demeanour and personality", suggesting that Manning needed a makeover. All three newspapers were highly critical of Manning's unwillingness to participate in a public debate with the opposition leader, and even more of his reasons for not doing so.

The editors were also disapproving of Manning's use of racial and religious rhetoric on the political platform to instil fears in his followers of being marginalized and discriminated against on the basis of ethnicity, should the balance of power shift to a government that was dominated by Indians and was predominantly Hindu. Prime Minister Manning warned supporters to be wary of the opposition leader's "own kind" (*Express*, 7 May 2010, 3), while insisting that Christians should be wary of the UNC under Makandal Daaga because he had desecrated the Roman Catholic Church during the Black Power Movement. Makandal Daaga was renowned in Trinidad and Tobago because he had led the movement in the 1970s, in which thousands of mostly black nationals protested against discrimination and racism.

The *Express* stated that Manning was "misstating fairly well-known events" (7 May 2010, 3), that "no such desecration occurred" and that he was "striving retroactively to make an artificial milestone out of a historical molehill". The newspaper was sceptical of Manning's claim that he was responsible for the harmonious relations among all ethnicities, describing his statement as "exaggerated, unbelievable and absurd". At the same time, the editor berated the UNC for using similar tactics in saying that "God was responsible for calling elections" and that "God wants Patrick Manning removed".

The editors were disapproving of Manning's political tactics, which appealed to a deep psychological fear between the two largest ethnic groups, a fear he was willing to exploit to retain power. They were also exasperated with the PNM's stunted development in the context of huge changes taking place in party politics within the UNC and national politics.

Although most of the editorials of the three newspaper were highly critical of Manning, in comparison, they were more even-handed and objective, and sometimes sympathetic, in their comments about Keith Rowley. An *Express* editorial praised Rowley for doing the country a great service by putting UDeCOTT firmly on the election agenda, stating that Rowley was Manning's "Achilles heel" (*Express*, 12 May 2010, 3), even though he had been ostracized for exposing corruption within his own party. *Newsday* was more sympathetic to Rowley, accusing the prime minister of "personal open animosity" and implying that he was "simply afraid of Rowley" because Rowley was a "stronger force". Even when Manning publicly supported Rowley's candidacy for the Diego Martin West seat, the *Newsday* editor used the opportunity to remind Rowley of all the wrongs Manning had perpetrated against him, such as having him "investigated, investigated, investigated ad nauseam" and calling him names such as "wajang" and "raging bull". Wajang is a local word used to describe a loud-mouthed, low character; "raging bull" is descriptive of someone out of control (18 April 2010, 3).

The public fight between Manning and Rowley was framed in a way that reflected negatively on the prime minister, portraying him to be a man who held personal grudges and vendettas against people who did not agree with him while showing up the weaknesses within the PNM structure.

Media Bias

The media were placed in the spotlight during the 2010 campaign because of allegations by the prime minister of media bias against both himself and his government. Even though it was the norm for politicians to accuse the media of biased reporting during elections, it was the first time in the ten years under review (2000–2010) that it became a platform issue in national politics. From early in the campaign, Prime Minister Manning attacked the media for not being fair, balanced or objective in their reporting (*Guardian*, 28 April 2010) and accusing them of focusing mostly on negatives concerning the PNM government (ibid.). He was supported by his minister of works and transport and the minister of information. The prime minister further charged that he was the "most vilified" prime minister the country had ever had, and that there were "elements that were ruthlessly monopolising the public information space to put us on a journey of spite and hate". Editors generally perceived this as an attack on press freedom and an attempt by the state to censor the media; for example, one *Newsday* editor viewed this as "an attack on the media", stating that "they make no apology for creating a space for the general public to debate the pressing issues of the day". He also reminded Manning that "everyone has the right to freedom of the press and other media of communication" (15 April 2010, 3).

The use of free time allocated in the private media to the state by the prime minister close to the election date confirmed to the media that the prime minister was making a "naked grab for power" and "using his State office to commander the free time allocated to government on the airwaves to give him an 'extraordinary advantage' over the opposition" (*Express*, 18 May 2010, 3). It further stated that Manning had "muscled into the spotlight" using strongman tactics. All three newspapers were vociferous about the use of state power to gain an unfair advantage over the PP in the crucial period leading up to the election. The fact was that this was part of the licensing agreement, which most governments chose to ignore. However, these charges and countercharges heightened the distrust between the government and the media and created a very hostile environment that made it difficult for both arms of the state to function effectively.

In interviews conducted with the media, most of them disagreed that they exhibited bias against Manning and his government. Sunity Maharaj-Best, a former editor of the *Express*, stated that this was a position adopted by every government whenever it felt overwhelmed by negative reporting during elections. This statement was endorsed by columnist Tony Fraser, who said this was typical of government in office: holding on to power and hitting out at the media. He further stated that all media were critical of government – and had every reason to be so. Andy Johnson, a former journalist with the *Express*, stated that media houses were generally too nervous about being seen as taking sides on political issues because of fear of what the political and business realities were in the country.

Crime

Throughout the campaign, the newspaper editors lamented the lack of adequate debate on governance issues, especially as related to the rising crime levels. This issue was very important, as successive administrations were not able to solve this problem, in addition to which, it was one of the issues Manning was heavily criticized for in the 2007 election, in which the media felt he had attempted to trivialize the problem. Editors were also critical of the UNC's position on crime, stating that its plans were cloudy and it was not treating it seriously, saying further that the UNC should come with "more concrete proposals" (*Express*, 18 May 2010, 3). In another editorial, the UNC was asked to "sharpen its focus because much of what was announced remained intangible" (*Express*, 4 April 2010, 3). Partial blame for the state of crime was placed on minister of national security Martin Joseph, who was described as someone "marked by consistent failure to get much right and who made opaque and recognisably inept statements" (*Express*, 25 April 2010, 3), as well as someone whose "lack of transparency compounds the blundering". In a later editorial, the *Express* editor stated that "the Minister of National Security remained one of the most ineffective in the outgoing Cabinet" (10 May 2010, 3).

Corruption

Corruption under the PNM regime was also a major concern to editors. One of the main issues that caught the attention of the editors was the premature end of parliament by the prime minister just when the Uff report was about to be debated. The Uff Commission was set up by the PNM to investigate allegations of corruption in bidding practices by state-owned UDeCOTT. It was felt that the report would have damaged the reputation of the prime minister and further eroded his credibility, and would lead to a "no-confidence" vote against him in the parliament.

Incensed by the prime minister's action, one editor stated that if the report had been debated in parliament, "it would disgrace Manning" (*Newsday*, 14 April 2010, 3). The editor further stated, "He needs to answer to no question on the Uff report as he campaigns before selected sycophant audiences, because no one will question him." Openly suggesting that Manning was hiding something, the editor stated, "It must not be allowed to disappear behind a smoke-screen of election rhetoric and political propaganda." So strongly did the editor feel about this subject that he stated, "We call upon all citizens and groups to keep the Uff report on the current agenda" (ibid.). On 4 May 2010, the editor repeatedly demanded that Manning explain his behaviour with regard to the Uff Commission and UDeCOTT, stating disdainfully that Manning's behaviour was "platitudinous at best and as a cynical cop-out at worst". He further insisted that Manning lacked integrity by not answering allegations of financial impropriety concerning the building of the church in Gunapo, a remote rural village in Trinidad. Manning was accused of using state funds to build a multimillion dollar church, called the Lighthouse of the Lord Jesus Christ, in the Heights of Gunapo in Trinidad for his spiritual adviser. The design for the building was originally slated for an extension in the prime minister's official residence. The editor also accused Manning of shielding himself with evasiveness, ambiguity and generalizations, exasperatingly stating, "Give us a break. You Mr Manning, are Prime Minister of the country and you must account to us. We don't have to prove anything" (*Newsday*, 14 May 2010, 3).

Coalition

Originally, the coalition was viewed with considerable scepticism and distrust by the editors, mainly because of the NAR experience in 1986 and Panday's "forced" attempts to unite the UNC with the COP in 2007. In an editorial on 18 April, the UNC leader, Persad-Bissessar, was called on to "clarify the accommodation" (*Guardian*, 18 April 2010, 3). The editorial expressed concerns about the way in which the accommodation was being handled, especially regarding the withholding of a document, the "Fyzabad Accord", signed at Charlie King Junction in Fyzabad on 21 April 2010 by the five political parties which made up the PP. Stating that she was fighting a war against disbelievers, the editor warned that Persad-Bissessar "must be aware that her battles are not only with the party in power but with the reservations and concerns of undecided voters". Still disbelieving, the editor described the accommodation as "a swiftly-stitched-together political animal" and a "new political coupling" between the UNC leader and the COP leader, Winston Dookeran. In a subsequent column, Tony Fraser questioned whether coalitions work and advised both that "it requires great maturity and wisdom" (*Guardian*, 21 April 2010, 3) and that it did not work in Trinidad because the former opposition leader, Basdeo Panday, was "a coalition-destroying presence". Editor Ken Ali described the accommodation as a "new trust and dream team as well as a people-oriented participatory government" (*Guardian*, 23 April 2010, 3). However, he warned the opposition leader to clear the air on the "ideological position" of union leaders, or else she could be "snatching defeat from the jaws of electoral victory". There were also instances when some columnists, such as Jai Parasram, used the opportunity to caution the opposition leader about her decisions. Parasram warned Persad-Bissessar to think carefully about bringing Justice Herbert Volney into the party, as it may "compromise the independence of the Judiciary" (*Guardian*, 30 April 2010, 3). Justice Volney resigned as a high court judge and immediately joined the UNC. Ken Ali further described Persad-Bissessar's action as "dangerous adventurism" and expressed concern that she should "so easily accept and embrace the practice of a high court judge walking into a camp". He then advised her "that it would be good to acknowledge an error without spinning it out of shape". In 2012, Justice Volney was expelled from the PP government.

Political Commentaries

Even though there was considerable scepticism regarding the coalition forces that came together, there was an underlying tone among columnists of optimism and hope about the impending change which would occur if the PP were to defeat the PNM. Tony Fraser wrote: "What seems certain is the need for change and transformation in the politics, the incorporation of all social and economic groups in the governance structure, and ending the reign of a leader who thinks he is ordained to rule" (*Guardian*, 19 May 2010, 28). Similarly, Anand Ramlogan stated, "We are at a critical crossroad in our development. This is our chance to reject the politics of the past and make a break for a new future. . . . Kamla's victory in the internal elections has inspired a quiet political revolution that will topple the old order" (*Guardian*, 23 May 2010, 29). Selwyn Ryan placed it in historical context as "a case of the 'old world' which was ushered in by Eric Williams in 1956 vs the new world which was coming into being and seeking political space to do its own thing. Patrick Manning symbolised the old world and Kamla the new" (*Express*, 23 May 2010, 13).

Not all columnists were as optimistic, Michael Harris warned that Persad-Bissessar "has no concept of what is required of her to play such a transformative role and has settled for the traditional role of leader of the opposition" (*Express*, 18 April 2010, 13). However, he continued, "We ought not to conclude . . . that the tremendous forces of change that were at work before the elections were called now cease to operate . . . the process of the collapse of the old regime will work itself through to its dire end and force us to the point where we either rise to the challenge of national transformation, beginning with the construction of a truly national party, or drink the bitter draughts of chaos" (ibid.).

Gender

The theme of gender in the 2010 general election was pervasive before the campaign period, when Persad-Bissessar decided to contest the UNC internal elections for party leadership against her mentor and founder of the UNC party, Basdeo Panday. Persad-Bissessar's affable personality easily won over the support of the women's arm of the UNC, as well as the Hindu Women's Organisation, in her effort to become the leader of the UNC. Following this, she gained national support from the female population in her bid to become the first female opposition leader. Persad-Bissessar recognized the importance of gender support in the election: "I am proud that my assumption to office can be an inspiration to women. . . . I am grateful for the immense support from women and women's groups across the country and to the extent that this helps to break the barriers so many competent women face" (*Newsday*, 23 May 2010, 13). Persad-Bissessar was also very popular among men in society, including journalists and columnists in the press, who continued to write positively about her. Given her rising popularity and cross-ethnic appeal, the media continued to position her as a viable contender for prime minister and the most likely candidate to unite the UNC with the COP. This process intensified when she emerged victorious in the UNC internal elections and started campaigning against the PNM in the lead-up to the general election. Rickey Singh wrote in the *Express*, "Kamla seems anxious to give meaning to a new political culture in [Trinidad and Tobago], a country too long stuck in the mud of race-based and men-led politics" (*Express*, 5 May 2010, 13).

Senior journalist Lennox Grant openly stated: "Much of the election 2010 politics is now a woman thing. . . . From behind the designer spectacles, the lady confronts a men's world of [Trinidad and Tobago] politics increasingly devoid of rules and of order" (*Express*, 2 May 2010, 13).

Race

The theme of race was less of a factor in the 2010 election, mostly because the media wanted to give the PP a chance to emerge while moving the dialogue away from race. In addition, the PP was not drawn along racial lines and attracted a diverse following. Race had always been a reality in Trinidad and Tobago's politics, especially as the PNM and the UNC's political bases were predominantly African and East Indian respectively. The media were also very tactful when reporting on racial slurs and slanders on the political platforms. On 13 April 2010, Prime Minister Manning, speaking on a PNM platform in St Augustine, told his audience that had they been on a UNC platform they would have heard, "Give me a Guinness and a puncheon", insinuating that East Indians were mostly involved in drinking large quantities of alcohol. The prime minister continued to attempt to instil racial fears within the African population by asking what portfolios would be given to "Prakash Ramadhar, Anand Ramlogan, Devant Maharaj, Tim Gopeesingh, Suruj Rambachan, and Austin 'Jack' Warner". Most of the names called were men of East Indian descent, with the exception of Warner, insinuating that Warner had betrayed his own people – those of African descent – by aligning with East Indians. Manning also suggested that government-funded programmes such as the Community-Based Environmental Protection and Enhancement Programme and the Government Assistance for Tuition Expenses Programme would be stopped once the UNC got into power, denying PNM party supporters employment and access to free tertiary education. These sentiments expressed by Manning further damaged the prime minister's credibility, while alienating East Indians within the PNM, as well as others who might have supported him during the 2010 election. It also adversely affected his reputation, which had already taken a beating because of his unpopular decisions and perceived arrogance.

Conclusion

The 2010 election was a highly publicized event in Trinidad and Tobago, with all three newspapers making the election the main topic of interest on their front pages over the course of the forty-five days of campaigning, with approximately 91 per cent of front pages reporting on the election. The *Guardian* gave it the most front pages, with almost 100 per cent coverage (98 per cent). The front pages focused heavily on photos relating to key people in the political parties, including the opposition leader and the prime minister. Most of the front pages comprised mostly headlines and large photos, with hardly any news stories. There was a greater propensity for all three newspapers to focus on group photos featuring politicians other than the two political leaders. When they did appear, however, the opposition leader was featured more times than the prime minister, and the photos of the opposition leader were much more positive than the photos of the prime minister. The headlines, in contrast, all focused mainly on the PNM, with most of them moving towards balanced reporting. However, a comparison of the number of negative headlines appearing on both the UNC and PNM revealed that there was a greater disposition to be negative towards the PNM.

Various personalities in the election were featured in the news stories, in all three newspapers, such as the PNM's Keith Rowley, Pennelope Beckles and Kennedy Swaratsingh, and in the PP, Winston Dookeran, Makandal Daaga, Ashworth Jack and Errol McLeod. However, when the two main political leaders, Kamla Persad-Bissessar and Patrick Manning, were featured, Manning appeared more times and was featured more negatively than Persad-Bissessar.

The actual governing of the country and some of the main issues such as crime were not as prominently featured by journalists covering the election as one might have expected. Reporters were more concerned with events as they unfolded on the platform, reporting generally on what was said by campaign speakers, who were mostly concerned with winning elections. Political platforms did not allow lengthy time to speak, which made it difficult for them to make any meaningful contribution. This is also reflected in reporters' framing the election as a contest between the PP and the PNM in the absence of serious issues being discussed. The media were viewed as sympathetic to the PP and hostile to the PNM, which spent considerable time fighting with them on the issue of bias. In this fiercely fought contest, political polls were used extensively to predict the outcome of the election, which may have inadvertently influenced the perceptions of voters. On the positive side, the media shied away from spending too much time on conflicts within the parties and among politicians. It can be concluded that the 2010 election was one in which traditional topics such as race and internal party bickering were not as important.

The slant of news stories was similar to that of the front pages, in that there was a tendency to be balanced in reporting on the day-to-day news on the campaign; however, when the newspapers did report on Manning, they were much more negative towards him than towards the UNC leader. News stories were written by reporters covering the campaign and were dependent on information that came mostly from politicians. Their reporting on what was said on the platform demonstrated that Manning bore the brunt of most of the rhetoric espoused by politicians on the PP platform and that he was generally spoken about negatively. However, Manning was featured more times than

Persad-Bissessar in terms of reporting what was said about him, indicating there was a structural bias in reporting news stories related to the election campaign that pertained to the prime minister. Further, there was structural bias in terms of sourcing information from the political leader of the PNM, which was reported in the press.

Both the editorials and political columnists of all three newspapers covered similar topics, using similar slants. There was general agreement across the three newspapers regarding key issues such as unity, change, gender, race, corruption and scandals, media bias, leadership under Manning and lack of meaningful debate on national issues such as crime, press freedom and integrity in public office. In some instances, there may have been more emphasis on particular issues by particular newspapers, but the issues focused on were, by and large, the same.

What has emerged from the analysis is that in the early stages of the campaign, there was uncertainty and scepticism regarding the coalition of disparate groups, parties and individuals, and perhaps some distrust. The theme of unity had been bandied about by consecutive political leaders in most elections in Trinidad and Tobago and was viewed as mere lip service by those aspiring to political office. Trinidad and Tobago politics had always been defined by the two major ethnic groups – East Indians and Africans – with East Indians voting for the UNC and Africans for the PNM. Each party had at times conveniently used unity to give the impression of inclusiveness of all races, but in general, this was viewed as superficial. Further, the NAR government of 1986, when the first coalition government was formed, had become highly unpopular because of the stringent fiscal policies it had to put into place because of the state of the economy and because of the early split which led to the formation of the UNC.

In addition, the formation of the PP under the umbrella of the UNC appeared to be hastily done to win the election. The composition of the group elicited distrust from certain segments of the media: it comprised the splintered COP, with its own ambitions of forming the government; the radical Black Power movement, led by national icon Makandal Daaga; the Tobago party, TOP, which had its own issues of insularity and island autonomy; and the trade-union-based Movement for Social Justice, which had traditionally been anti-establishment, espousing socialist ideology and the rhetoric to go with it. From the outset, it was difficult to imagine that a lone woman would be able to rein in the ambitions of the powerful men who headed these organizations and to be considered their leader. Beyond that, the Fyzabad Accord which was signed by the five polical parties which comprised the PP, seemed to be shrouded in mystery, with the media not having access to information regarding the terms and conditions that were agreed on. Repeated calls to have the document disclosed went unheeded, creating further uncertainty and scepticism. Eventually, it was published by the press.

However, Persad-Bissessar emerged at a time when major changes were taking place within the country, as well as regionally and internationally. Here in Trinidad, with the disenchantment with male-dominated politics and the deadlock held by the PNM and UNC, women especially were willing to throw their support behind a capable woman, with the hope of seeing a new kind of leadership in both party and government. The changes happening within and outside of Trinidad and Tobago set the stage for Persad-Bissessar and the coalition to emerge as a political force.

Newsday, which was headed by a woman, openly supported Persad-Bissessar, and appeared to be positive in its coverage and negative towards the leadership of the PNM. As the campaign progressed, the media appeared to have bought into the PP, with editorials and commentaries moving towards more positive coverage. Questions were still being raised, but the tone of the writing shifted, adding more references to change and transformation. The country was beginning to hope for changed politics once again, which was reflected as editors and columnists called for the transformation of politics and leadership in their newspapers. Editors and columnists were willing to give the coalition a chance, with the hope it would lead to a new kind of national politics. They deliberately sidelined issues such as race and conflict, choosing to focus on the PP and the business of governance instead.

Although the press was supportive of the PP, in contrast, it was disapproving of the authoritarian style of the PNM political leader, which many found antithetical to democracy. Fiercely protective of its rights to freedom of the press enshrined in Trinidad and Tobago's constitution and its role as "watchdogs" of democracy, and deeply resentful of his accusations of media bias against his party and government, the press became critical of Manning's evasiveness, brashness and arrogance in addressing critical issues such as the Uff report, the UDeCOTT scandal, the mismanagement of the economy, the wastage of public funds on large projects, and the use of state funds to build a private church. *Newsday* was highly critical of his lack of integrity in public office and his personal vendetta against PNM loyalist Keith Rowley. Manning's actions placed him on the wrong side of the media, and although he gained much press coverage, it was mostly negative. This had a downward-spiralling effect on his image, causing him to become highly unpopular with both the media and the population. This may very well have rubbed off on the PNM, resulting in the party's losing favour and popularity.

It can be concluded that most of the editors and columnists of all three newspapers exhibited partisan bias towards the PP, having embraced the ideology of change and transformation under a new political structure. At the same time, they openly rejected the PNM under the leadership of Patrick Manning. However, editors and columnists were not as critical of the PNM as a party so much as its leader, as indicated by their sympathy for Keith Rowley and Pennelope Beckles, both of whom were considered contenders for the leadership of the PNM and were viewed as having been ostracized from the party by the PNM leader.

CHAPTER 7

Findings Based on a Comparative Study of Five Elections

THE INTENT OF THIS BOOK WAS TO EXAMINE the relationship between press and politics in political campaigns in Trinidad and Tobago during a volatile political period in the country's history, from 2000 to 2010, in which five elections were called in ten years. The objectives were to explore whether the local daily newspapers exhibited partisan or structural bias in their coverage of political news during the campaign periods through varied writings. A further objective was to determine whether media bias was a major factor in election coverage, so as to gain a better understanding of the role the print media play in political campaigns and to address possible solutions to strengthen both the independent role of the media and the democratic process in a small island state such as Trinidad and Tobago, while making a case for a new model of media and politics.

Framing the Political Agenda

The personality frame was by far the most dominant frame used by journalists when reporting on political news, indicating general interest in politicians, and especially the leadership of political parties and the country. These personalities came from the UNC, the PNM and the PP.

Basdeo Panday, Patrick Manning and Kamla Persad-Bissessar were the dominant leaders of the country during the decade under study. However, of all the politicians placed on the front covers, the UNC, PNM and PP political leaders were featured most, with a preference towards featuring the incumbent

Table 19. Frames for 2000–2010 Elections

Year	Issue	Personality (Panday)	Personality (Manning)	Other Politicians	Govern-ing	Conflict	Horse Race
2000	311	336	256	205	11	45	371
2001	523	779	335	2,190	52	338	338
2002	458	211	258	539	41	132	291
2007	132	192	324	1,177	58	149	134
2010[*]	865	522	865	1,208	325	391	920

[*]In 2010 Panday was replaced by Persad-Bissessar in the Personality frame.

prime minister and the opposition leader, mostly together rather than singly, on the covers.

However, when the media did feature the political leaders alone, the prime minister, regardless of which party he or she represented, was featured more times than the opposition leader, with the exception of 2010, when opposition leader Kamla Persad-Bissessar was featured more than the prime minister on the covers of the *Guardian* and *Newsday*. Persad-Bisssessar had become a political celebrity following the UNC's internal elections in January 2010, after successfully challenging the founding leader to emerge as the first woman to head a political party in a traditionally male-dominated profession. Other factors also contributed to her placement on the front covers, such as her news value as a novelty as a female challenger for the post of prime minister, together with her genuine attempts at forming a coalition grouping that was more representative of the diverse population and interests of the country, and that, if successful, posed a serious threat to the existing government. In contrast, Prime Minister Manning had become highly unpopular because of allegations of corruption and scandals that were worsened by internal party fighting and attacks on the media, claiming biased reporting. Further, Manning's unpopular policy initiatives, together with his perceived arrogance, contributed to his declining popularity.

Issue frames declined considerably from 2000 to 2007, falling very low in priority for journalists when compared with personality frames. However, in 2010, there was increased interest in issues when compared with the 2000–2007 period, although use of the issue frame was much lower when compared with the personality frame. During the decade, the discourse remained focused on a limited number of topics, such as the election process and the role of the EBC in conducting fair elections, rising criminality and media bias, to name a few. High on the political agenda were scandals and corruption that surrounded the party in power, whether the UNC or PNM, contributing to general negativity among the public about all governing parties. This penchant of the press to focus on a limited number of topics was reflective of the limited range of topics discussed on political platforms by the opposing parties. The combative style of campaigning by both governing and opposition parties, in which leaders of the political parties were under attack, limited the number and range of topics discussed and reported in the newspapers. Very little discussion was given to issues pertaining to governance, especially those with regional and international implications. This has had a deleterious effect on the citizenry by limiting information and discussion on issues of national, regional and international importance and trivializing the democratic process, while increasing public cynicism towards politicians.

Conflict frames were used strategically during the 2000–2010 period. The press demonstrated considerable maturity in the way it reported on conflicts during the ten-year period, choosing not to focus overly on personal conflicts while redirecting the dialogue to issues worthy of national discussion. However, during times of close calls between the governing and opposition parties, the conflict frame was applied to magnify certain conflicts, which worked against unpopular leaders and their parties, as seen with the Panday and Manning regimes. When the conflicts were between the media and certain politicians, the media generally magnified the conflicts in their favour and this worked against certain regimes and governments. Panday's fight with both Persad-Bissessar and Dookeran over succession issues during the UNC's internal election before the 2010 general election was published to give the impression that Panday was combative and conflict-prone; both Dookeran and Persad-Bissessar were framed as more suitable alternative leaders. The extension of that conflict to certain journalists and media houses contributed to the negative framing and unpopularity of Panday. Similarly, the conflict between Manning and Rowley was magnified in the lead-up to the 2010 election and contributed to the rising unpopularity of Manning as a leader, distinct from the PNM party; Rowley was framed as a more suitable leader for that party. Both Panday and Manning were replaced as political leaders of the UNC and PNM in 2010. One can conclude that the strategic use of the conflict frame during close elections, especially when conflict included the media, together with the declining popularity of a leader, could position political leaders and parties negatively, adversely affecting their chances at the polls during elections.

The horse-race frame was moderately used during the five elections (2000–2010), indicating general indifference and disenchantment with the election process and the actual outcome of the elections with the exception of 2010, when there was a strong possibility the coalition movement would change the party structure, and thus break the deadlock held by the two traditional parties (the UNC and PNM) and their leaders during the decade under study. National interest reached an all-time high in the 2010 election, as evidenced by the huge volume of coverage given to that election. One can conclude that the number and frequency of elections, at an average of one every two years from 2000 to 2010, had resulted in an election-weary population grown cynical about the election process, the deadlock held by the two traditional parties and the actual outcome of the elections.

Unity and coalition frames were the least popular frames used by journalists when reporting on elections. It was only during the 2010 campaign, when it appeared that coalition attempts were genuine under the PP, that the press focused its attention on the governing frame; even so, this was done moderately when compared with the use of personality frames. This was not surprising, as journalists had grown highly suspicious and distrustful of coalition attempts after the NAR experience of 1986. Independent postcolonial societies have been known to concentrate overly on issues such as race and unity, while paying little attention to other national issues. However, the shifting of attention away from these themes should be viewed as a positive development for media and politics in Trinidad and Tobago and as demonstrating a concerted attempt by the media to focus on more relevant issues of governance.

Watchdogs of Democracy

During the ten-year period, the editorials of all three dailies were highly opinionated about similar issues, such as leadership of the country and issues of governance relating to the conduct of free and fair elections by the EBC; the politicizing of state institutions, such as the police service; the prevalence of corruption among government officials; high crime rates; and accusations of media bias. Editors were also strong champions of freedom of the press and the role of the media and openly condemned any attacks on the integrity of the journalistic profession. Editors of all three dailies took their role as watchdogs very seriously, mediatizing (Bennett and Entman 2001) the political communication process between the political directorate and the citizenry by insisting on accountability, transparency and integrity in public office. In most instances, editors were generally harsh on incumbent governments and their leaders; for example, during the short period Panday was prime minister, from 2000 to 2002, his government was heavily criticized by the editors for corruption. Manning was also placed under the microscope in 2007 and 2010, during his tenure as prime minister, because of his inability to keep crime down. Manning's propensity to forge alliances with criminal elements in the society also drew harsh criticism from editors of the three newspapers. Both leaders responded to the media by accusing them of biased reportage, which resulted in deteriorating government and media relations, making it very difficult for the government and the media to function effectively together in the interest of democracy.

Public Sphere for Open Discussion

Commentaries were usually written by a combination of personalities who were knowledgeable on issues of governance, such as political scientists from the University of the West Indies, people who had served in government or senior public-service positions, heads of religious organizations, lawyers, trade unionists and representatives of political parties and other social interest groups. A very small group was drawn from the journalistic profession. The views expressed by this diverse group of writers mostly represented their own thinking or that of their organizations and, in most instances, were separate from those expressed by editors of newspapers. Sympathizers and supporters of particular political parties who wrote columns generally declared their partisanship.

However, there were similarities in the themes addressed by columnists of all three dailies regarding the leadership and governance styles of political leaders, race relations, ethics and gender. During the five elections, one of the major themes addressed by columnists was that of leadership of the country. Editors were very concerned about the growing authoritarianism demonstrated by political leaders of both the UNC and the PNM, which they interpreted as creeping dictatorship. Columnists were of the view that both Manning and Panday had, over the years, demonstrated autocratic tendencies – holding on to power at all costs – and as result, were antagonistic to any attempts to make them accountable to the electorate.

Sidelining Racial Rhetoric during Campaigns

Race had always been a major factor in Trinidad and Tobago elections, with support drawn from the two largest ethnicities to form the bases of the PNM and UNC parties. During the ten years under review, the issue of race became less of a factor in the political commentaries and all but disappeared from the discourse in 2010. In general, the discussion on race was handled very sensitively by most columnists, although the newspapers did allow certain columnists who felt strongly on the topic ample space to air their views. These columnists were mostly East Indians who wrote about the marginalization and alienation of this ethnic group as a result of what they regarded as the deliberate discriminatory policies of the PNM government. The marginalization of East Indians was directly related to the longevity of governance by the PNM. One school of thought was that each group, when in power, tended to favour its own ethnic group, and because the PNM had been the longest-serving government, with the UNC and NAR each being one-term parties, the balance of power had mostly been in favour of Africans in terms of state patronage.

In addition, there was a correlation between race relations and party politics. Under the existing Westminster model, the two-party system resulted in a majoritan government in which the winner-takes-all structure pervades. From 2000 to 2007, both the PNM and UNC had their turn at government, with the spoils of government going mainly to their supporters. As a result, over the course of ten years of governance, both ethnicities felt marginalized and alienated at different periods; this was excerbated by the quick turnover of elections, in which an average of one election was called every two years. An election-weary populace had grown tired of leaders exploiting race to further divide the country, and this was reflected in the political commentaries by columnists who deliberately sidelined this issue while being highly critical of political leaders for using race to incite their supporters during campaigns.

By 2007, when the political landscape shifted to include a third party, the COP, and in 2010, a new entity, the PP, that embraced all opposition parties, the discourse on race had dwindled significantly, almost disappearing completely. The new coalition movement created a structure that did not depend on one ethnic group for support but had an inclusive policy that involved diverse groups that were more representative of Trinidad and Tobago's mosaic society. Therefore, the sensitivity in terms of the political discourse on race reflected in columns was very much in tune with the thinking on the ground, while showing a deliberate attempt by columnists to redirect the thinking of the citizenry on the basis of this traditional theme. This is a positive step in the development of politics and media in Trinidad and Tobago, in which evidence points to columnists deliberatively trying to shift the discourse away from traditional themes of race and feelings of alienation and marginalization based on ethnicity and to raise the political discourse to a higher level to include governance issues.

Evidence of Structural and Partisan Bias in Newspapers

In general, the press tried to be even-handed and objective in its reportage during political campaigns over the course of the ten years under review. However, there was a general tendency to frame incumbent prime ministers and their governments negatively, whether UNC or PNM. The intensity of negativity differed each election year; for example, Panday was consistently framed negatively because of allegations of corruption and scandals starting early in 2000, when he was prime minister, that followed him right down to the end of his political career. Similarly, Manning became very unpopular in 2010, also because of allegations of corruption and scandals. In contrast, the COP's political leader, Winston Dookeran, and the UNC leader, Kamla Persad-Bissessar, were both framed more positively by the local press in 2007 and 2010 respectively. Both were opposition leaders at the time, indicating partisan bias by the press towards new leaders under a more representative party system in which race and ethnicity were not major factors. Evidence points to both structural and partisan bias against the Panday-led government from 2000 to 2002 by all three dailies, especially the *Express*, as Panday was consistently portrayed negatively by the papers.

The bias against Panday appeared to have originated from a personal conflict with the chief executive officer of the *Express*, Ken Gordon, which ended up in the courts. Both Panday and Gordon were cabinet ministers in the NAR government in 1986; a bitter conflict in the party resulted in Panday leaving the coalition to form his own party, Club 88, which became the UNC. Gordon, in contrast, was appointed a senator and minister of industry, enterprise and tourism by then-prime minister A.N.R. Robinson. Gordon had remained in the NAR government after Panday left, but soon after returned to the media to head the CCN group of companies, which owned the *Express*. In 1995, the UNC government, under the leadership of Panday, won the national election. In 1997, Panday's government introduced a Green Paper on media reform; Gordon responded negatively on behalf of the media fraternity, describing it as "Machiavellian", resulting in Panday's calling Gordon a "pseudo-racist" (Gordon 1999).

The ongoing battle between the *Express* and Panday became highly personalized in 2000, when Panday blamed the United Kingdom's press for the death of Diana, Princess of Wales. The press in Trinidad and Tobago regarded this comment as a desire to curb press freedom and became defensive of their rights, enshrined in the constitution (Constitution of Trinidad and Tobago, 1976). By 2001, the *Express*'s insistence on framing the Panday-led government as corrupt had angered Panday to the extent that he led an onslaught on TV6, a subsidiary of CCN, which also owned the *Express*, describing the station in the most vitriolic terms. By 2007, the relationship between Panday and the *Express* had degenerated drastically, with personal insults flying back and forth between editors and Panday.

The personal fight between these two headstrong and powerful personalities, one from business/media and the other from politics, with its genesis in politics, was played out in the public sphere over the course of two decades and had considerable influence over editorial policy in the choice, slant and tone of topics published in the *Express*. In a small society such as Trinidad and Tobago, in which various media fed off each other, it is likely that the editorial policy of the *Express* would also have influenced the editorial policies of the other two dailies, as demonstrated by the overall negativity towards Panday in both the *Guardian* and *Newsday*.

The structural bias against the political leader of the UNC also influenced the negative framing of the UNC party and the preference shown to alternative parties, the COP and the PP, with portrayals of them as more attractive parties for governing the country. Faced with opposition by both the editors and owners of newspapers and alienated by the press, which he interpreted as bias against his government, Panday found himself in a most difficult situation, resulting in his accusing the *Express* of plotting to bring down his government.

Although from 2002 to 2007, editors addressed the issue of governance under the leadership of Patrick Manning, focusing on his inability to solve the increasing crime problem and his linkages with local criminals, it was in 2010, when Manning's popularity declined tremendously, that the slant and tone of editorials and commentaries became more negative towards him. However, the negativity towards the PNM leader was not directed towards the entire PNM party; the editors were much more positive about a former deputy political leader, Keith Rowley, framing him as a more suitable leader for the party. Similarly, the political leader's accusations of media bias only worsened relations between Manning and the established press.

In 2007 and 2010 respectively, preference was shown for both the COP and the PP by columnists of all three daily newspapers, who portrayed the parties as more attractive, new leadership to govern the country. Editors were more circumspect in their opinions concerning these two new parties in the political landscape and tended to be much more cautious in their writing, although the subtext suggested hopefulness for the possibility of new governance.

In contrast, columnists were much more opinionated in their writing, with many of them openly supporting these two new parties. In 2010, when Persad-Bissessar became a serious contender for prime ministership, women across the country supported her because they felt that for the first time a woman could shatter the glass ceiling. Also during this time, other female leaders had achieved prime ministerial and presidential status around the world. The winds of change in terms of reversal of gender roles and equity in male–female relationships were sweeping the world, and Trinidad and Tobago became swept up in the euphoria of the moment. Columnists, both men and women, who were tracking Persad-Bissessar's career threw their support behind the lone woman, seeing the potential for her to emerge as a national leader and the most likely candidate to lead a unified force against the incumbent and long-standing PNM government. Although internationally, the press tends to objectify women in the way they are framed, Persad-Bissessar was glorified by a highly benevolent press who raised her to celebrity status, which gave her an edge over her competitors. The objectification of Persad-Bissessar was done mostly by her colleagues within the UNC during its internal elections in January 2010, and by the PNM during the 2010 campaign.

It may well be that a built-in bias or preference in the society for a departure from "old politics" (since 2006, the COP had campaigned on the premise of "new politics") represented by the older political leaders had surfaced. The new leader of the UNC, Persad-Bissessar, and the leader of the COP, Dookeran, having broken away from the old UNC, represented something different. The coalition of five political parties also represented something new. The yearning for something new and fresh by the population may well have reflected itself in the press, both in tangible press coverage and in spirit. The freshness of a female leader in a male-dominated political arena and the prospect of the country's first female prime minister may also have coalesced in a kind of national yearning, which at once was reflected in the press to the extent that the press became advocates for change as well. At the same time, the negativity that surrounded the then governing party and its "old" leader made it difficult to present Manning and his ruling party in a positive light. The dynamic between public opinion's influencing the press and the press's influencing public opinion may have been mutually reinforcing.

Bias as a Factor in the Outcome of National Elections

There were two surges of increased volume in political coverage over the course of the five campaign periods; during the 2002 (58.1 per cent) and 2010 (91.11 per cent) campaigns, both incumbent governments, the UNC and PNM, were beaten at the polls, and new governments formed. In general, press coverage of elections averaged around 50 per cent of newspaper content. These two media-driven campaigns resulted in changed governments in 2002 and 2010 respectively, suggesting the press may have played an important role in the outcome of at least two elections, even if this meant positioning leaders by framing them in a particular way or reinforcing existing opinions about political parties and candidates. In Trinidad and Tobago, the media may have reinforced in the minds of the voting public that both the UNC and PNM governments in 2002 and 2010 respectively had run their course and that re-election of these parties, at the particular times in question, was not in the best interest of the country.

The fact remains that over the course of the ten years under review, five elections were held, in which evidence points to an active media role in which political campaigns became highly mediatized (Bennett and Entman 2001), with a tendency for the press to focus on incumbent governments, using corruption and scandals to frame consecutive leaders. In a young democracy such as Trinidad and Tobago, five elections could not have been called without the intervention of the media, and evidence points to the fall of at least two governments as a result of the role of the press.

Two key issues are being argued in this particular instance. Although structural bias or partisan bias may not demonstrate in a crass form the shift in the frame of emphasis from the traditional personality and horse-race frames to the conflict frame, they may well have functioned to structure and influence the thinking of the electorate. In 2007, the media bias was strong enough to cast doubt on the efficacy of the current ruling party. In 2007, it was not enough to cause a shift away from the traditional leadership and their parties, even in the wake of a party's espousing new politics and new leadership. In any case, the conflict frame was not dominant in this election. In 2010, although the conflict frame could have been highlighted in the case of the coalition PP, it was not. Yet, when the conflict frame included conflict with the media, as demonstrated during Panday's reign in 2000–2002 and Manning's governance in 2010, the election resulted in both parties' being defeated at the polls. To this extent, the application of the conflict frame in the presentation of political parties does seem to be an influential factor, if not the decisive factor, in the determination of election outcomes.

Conclusion

The traditional role as disseminators of information is still very much part of the nation's newspapers' routine function, as journalists report on news events as they occur daily. In contrast, the voices of editors and columnists have also been instrumentalized to act as watchdogs of the country's democracy, keeping politicians in check by insisting on accountability, transparency and integrity in public life. The diversity of this group was represented in the pluralistic views expressed in columns during the decade studied. During 2000–2010, topics tended to be similar, with politicians focusing on corruption, scandals and the electioneering process, and with little attention being paid to national issues of governance. In addition, reporters were very careful in managing personal conflicts between opposing politicians while trying to move the national dialogue away from traditional themes such as race and unity by focusing on issues of national governance. Framing was focused mostly on the political personalities, especially the leadership of parties. The heavy focus on politicians as sources of information by daily reporters covering the campaigns resulted in structural bias by those newspapers, and evidence points to partisan bias towards new political parties, which were more representative of the diversity of the country.

CHAPTER 8

A Way Forward for Media and
Politics in Trinidad and Tobago

THE ROLE OF THE DAILY PRESS IN POLITICAL campaigns in Trinidad and Tobago has
become increasingly important in politics during the last decade, evolving from
intermediaries of information to mediatization (Strömbäck and Esser 2014) in
the political communication process between governments and the citizenry
within which the "watchdog" role has evolved. The press has grown stronger
as a professional sector during the decade under review (2000–2010); even
though it still has far to go in terms of becoming the proverbial "fourth estate"
within the existing paradigm of the democratic system in post-independence
politics of Trinidad and Tobago. The strengthening of the institutions of both
media and politics therefore has implications for the growth and development
of a healthy democracy and augurs well for good governance of the country.

The quest for something new, fresh and pure in politics seems to be a yearning for new parties that was reflected by certain columnists. However, the
manner in which certain columnists wrote was at times construed as "attack
journalism" and was open to accusations of "bias" by politicians and the voting public. In a country in which conspiracy theories abound, it was difficult
to convince those at the wrong end of the pen that certain columnists meant
well and had no hidden agenda. By casting most political aspirants in both
government and opposition negatively, the press has increased public cynicism
towards political leaders and the political process, resulting in more eligible
voters deciding not to vote. During close elections, the undecideds and new
voters are the ones who hold the balance of power in their hands.

The type of journalism practised has also affected the number and type of people who have offered themselves up for public office, with implications for the governance of the country. The presidentalization of elections, with its heavy focus on the personality and personal lives of political leaders, has had a bruising effect on those who have put themselves up for public office, wishing to contribute to the development of the society. Women in particular have been reluctant to enter into politics, and as a result, the field of politics continues to be dominated by men.

Evidence points to the press having an increasingly stronger effect on electoral outcomes because of the manner in which it frames particular parties, politicians and issues. Further, it may have actually precipitated the early calling of elections before they were constitutionally due by magnifying and intensifying media coverage of conflicting situations, especially when these conflicts involved the media and political leaders. This was especially true of those prime ministers who were openly combative towards the media and in situations in which press/politics relations had become openly hostile, as found with the Panday (2000–2002) and Manning (2007–2010) regimes. These issues, however, are further complicated by the dynamic interactions among citizen views, press response to these views and the response of citizens to news and views presented in the press; this, in turn, influenced public opinion.

In a small country such as Trinidad and Tobago, in which the media system is small and limited in resources, it is a norm for incumbent governments and their political leaders to be considered leading experts on government policy and to be the main sources of information for journalists performing their duties. The "presidentalization" (Hallin and Mancini 2004) of political campaigns, as found in Trinidad and Tobago, is common in democracies around the world, including those of larger developed countries, as well as Latin America and the Caribbean. However, opposition leaders rarely make news unless they are involved in controversies or conflicts that directly affect governance.

Newspapers, by and large, are private businesses concerned with selling newspapers for profit, and will generally focus on who or what makes news daily. Given that the government is the largest advertiser in the country, owners of newspapers are very careful during campaign periods to manage their publications so as not to alienate either party, especially when they are uncertain about the outcome of elections. The heavy focus on government politicians as sources of information has resulted in a structural bias towards politicians and governing parties in news stories; this is compounded by journalistic norms and practices. In addition, the lack of experience and proper training of young reporters, together with the urgency of producing material for publication, has resulted in a heavy focus on government officials as the main sources of information.

Political Parallelism between Media and Politics

Given the peculiarities of Trinidad and Tobago's society, with a current population of only 1.3 million individuals, in which most people in media, politics and business know each other, evidence points to strong political parallelism (Hallin and Mancini 2004) between journalists and politicians, with the latter being considered the most important source of political information. In interviews conducted with nine seasoned media practitioners in Trinidad and Tobago in November 2011, most of the journalists indicated that one of their primary sources of information was politicians, and that relationships with politicians were important for this purpose. So in addition to normal sources of information, such as press conferences, private individuals and other media, the politician himself was a major source of information; thus, cultivation of relationships with politicians by journalists was an important consideration in honing a journalistic competitive edge. This dependence on a source that represents the status quo or bourgeoisie in society creates an "establishment bias" in reportage, as it represents the views of one particular group of people.

This closeness between politicians and media professionals in Trinidad and Tobago is demonstrated in the crossing-over of media professionals into the realm of politics, especially at the end of an election campaign, aptly described as a "revolving door" between the professions. After an election, journalists sometimes end up with senior positions on state boards, ministries and especially in state-owned media. With changes in party power, journalists in government often return to the media as well. The movement of media practitioners from privately owned media houses to state-owned media in the aftermath of elections is not an unusual phenomenon in Trinidad and Tobago. Depending on the government in power, these positions usually last for five years or longer, as was the case of the PNM government, which has been the longest-serving government. In some instances, politicians who have been at the losing end of politics have entered the media domain as columnists, becoming opinion leaders and writing extensively on issues relating to governance and politics.

The strong political parallelism that exists between the state and the media, which generally employed people of different political orientations, has blurred the lines between politicians and media practitioners. On one hand, politicians are under the impression that their close alliances with certain media practitioners can influence the agenda of newspapers in favour of their party. The media, on the other hand, even while working with allies in government to provide scoops and to source information, insist on maintaining their professionalism, independence and the right to press freedom enshrined in the constitution. However, these close relationships, cultivated over time by media professionals and politicians alike, have made journalists and their media houses vulnerable to allegations of bias. On the positive side, they have created more aggressive self-censorship by editors and media managers in the newsroom. Editors and other media professionals who have compromised the profession are themselves the brunt of media censure by their own colleagues and are forced to desist from these practices.

Maintaining Balance in the Interest of Democracy

The dependence of highly influential private media on state resources provided via advertising revenues has created a symbiotic relationship between the government and private media in which a delicate balance must be maintained for both to function effectively in the interest of the country. Traditionally, newspapers' owners are from the private sector and can exert considerable influence and pressure over the political system by influencing public opinions and giving voice to disenfranchised groups in society. By instrumentalizing these voices, such as the trade unions, religious organizations, academics and opposition forces, the press could exert considerable pressure on governments. At the same time, the state can exert considerable power over private media because it is the largest advertiser in the country, and the media are dependent on revenues derived from state advertising to survive. Media houses run as businesses for the purpose of generating profits and the press as an independent organization can sometimes create conflict between media owners and editors and influence what is actually published in newspapers. When one takes into consideration competition from online media and the expansion of the media system through the granting of more licences, the integrity of the printed media may be compromised even further to keep newspapers afloat.

Added to this complexity is the blurring of lines between politics and media, with the rotation of professionals through both fields and the deep social connections, personal relationships and networks formed between politicians and people in the press over long periods of time. The smallness of the country makes it impossible not be connected to someone through familial or business relations. A further layer of complexity is added by the smallness of the media system, which is controlled by a group of practitioners rotating and interchanging from one media house to another. Personal grudges and partisan biases against politicians and political parties can easily be transferred from one media house to another and become viral throughout the profession. Likewise, political grudges against certain media practitioners and houses can remain dormant when a party is out of office, only rearing their heads when the party returns to the corridors of power. Unfortunately for media houses, those working journalists who have been actively involved in politics are considered to be "politically tainted" and are rarely considered objective and independent journalists by the reading public, ultimately negatively affecting public perception of certain media houses.

What has emerged out of this study is that there is a link between the system of media in Trinidad and Tobago and the output of content, based on heavy dependence on sourcing information mostly from politicians active in government, which sets the national agenda by limiting conversation and discussion around a few carefully selected topics. Evidence points to structural bias towards political regimes, regardless of political parties, as found with the UNC and PNM during their respective reigns. Further, there is an institutional bias against governments while in office, as demonstrated by the propensity to be negative towards all governments and political leaders while being much more positive to new opposition parties, leading to what might be called the incumbency disadvantage. Evidence also points to partisan bias towards parties that are considered more representative of the diverse interests and political reality of Trinidad and Tobago, in which ethnicity and race are gradually disappearing in the background as people become more informed and educated about politics and their expectations of political parties and politicians continue to grow.

The national discourse is changing, somewhat slowly, away from postcolonial themes such as unity, and there is less interest in personal conflicts as the country demands accountability, transparency and good governance from its political leaders. Although the press's interventionist role has had some success in terms of increasing interest in the democratic traditions of the country, as evidenced by the dramatic increase in the volume of coverage in 2010, it has created a combustible environment between the press and politicians that could erupt at the smallest provocation. It does not augur well for the country if the free media only report on negativity surrounding incumbent governments while ignoring the positives that have evolved from policy initiatives in the interest of the citizenry of the country; neither does it augur well for the state to threaten to shut down media houses by withholding resources or by trying to influence its supporters not to purchase newspapers.

A delicate balance, without compromising the roles of the state and the press, needs to be maintained between press and politics for both to function effectively in the interest of democracy. For this to be achieved, a certain level of maturity must be exercised on both sides, with each acknowledging their separate but mutually reinforcing roles and responsibilities within the existing democratic system. This is by no means a proposition for developmental journalism, in which the free media act as the public-relations machinery for the state (this function is left to the state media, of which there are a number in the country) but, instead, is a proposition for a way forward for media and politics. In extreme cases, governments can become patriarchal centres of power, and government public relations can morph into the systematic output of propaganda with effective machinery to support it. This book instead makes a case for a working relationship between the free media and the state, recognizing that each has a role in the country's development as we move from developing to developed status in the world economy.

Therefore, both press and politics must find a zone of common ground in which to operate and to ease the tensions between the various estates in the governance process without inhibiting the capacity of each estate to play its legitimate and constitutional role, recognizing that the existing parliamentary system and the political culture it has facilitated in a plural society has already created a highly adversarial system of politics.

Gendered Media and Politics

The role of women in media and politics has changed dramatically in the post-independence era, with the ascendency of Kamla Persad-Bissessar as the first female prime minister in the country in 2010 and the heading of the three local daily newspapers, the *Guardian, Express* and *Newsday*, exclusively by women. Persad-Bissessar must be credited for shattering stereotypical notions of the role of women in a traditionally patriarchal society, after decades of colonialism and male authoritarian leadership. Female editors must also be credited for being vociferous "watchdogs of democracy", holding governments and their leaders accountable despite the fact that a woman had become prime minister.

Women have found a new confidence with the appointment of the first female prime minister, who has been able to crack the proverbial "glass ceiling" to achieve the highest office. Women's issues are being given more credence and more women have been given opportunities to serve in public. Prime Minister Persad-Bissessar also showed sensitivity to the plight of disadvantaged women in society and has implemented a number of programmes to assist them, such as a baby-care grant for pregnant women, the Children's Life Fund and the construction of a children's hospital.

Persad-Bissessar's rise from party politics to emerge as the first female leader of a traditionally male-dominated party, to national politics and to leading the country was not without its challenges. She was vilified within her own party and was portrayed in the most negative terms. Her tenure as prime minister was heavily scrutinized and criticized by both her opponents and some elements of the media, with much emphasis on her leadership capabilities. In a country accustomed to authoritarian, male leaders, her collaborative approach within the PP has been perceived as a weakness by some.

The treatment of the first female prime minister has implications for the role of women in politics in the future. Women who have witnessed the personal onslaught against, character assassination of and invasion of the privacy of the prime minister will be more reluctant to contribute to the development of the country through politics. Already, the executive and parliament have unequal proportions of women to men and continue to be dominated by men.

The period 2000–2010 also saw the rise of women in key positions in the newsrooms, with more women also being hired as journalists. In 2012, all three dailies were headed by female editors-in-chief, Judy Raymond at the *Guardian*, Omatie Lyder at the *Express* and Therese Mills at *Newsday* respectively. Both the *Express* and *Newsday* have been consistent in their promotion of women to key positions in their newspapers. Sunity Maharaj-Best, former editor-in-chief of the *Express*, gained a reputation as a hard-hitting journalist and columnist much feared by politicians, and other female journalists such as Camini Marajh and Therese Mills have also gained a reputation for their work; in 2006 and 2012 respectively they were granted honorary doctorates from the University of the West Indies for their contributions to the field of journalism.

It is noteworthy that even though the highest offices in media and politics were held by women during the period under study, relations between these two important estates continued to be strained. It is worth considering whether female editors and journalists are harder on female politicians because their expectations are higher and their disappointment greater when these expectations are not met. However, the rise of women in government and media demonstrates that women can function and lead at the highest levels and can govern in the interest of democracy of the country.

A New Model of Media and Politics

There is no existing model that best describes the reality of media and politics as practised in a small developing country, such as Trinidad and Tobago, in the post-independence period, in which freedom of the press is enshrined in the constitution, thereby setting the framework for the growth and development of the free media. Trinidad and Tobago has gradually moved from a system of authoritarianism (Siebert, Paterson and Schramm 1956), prevalent during the period of colonialism, in which the state media dominated the media landscape, to a more liberal system in the post-independence period. Significant progress was achieved in 1986, when the regime then in power, the NAR, deregulated the monopoly held by the state media and increased the number of licences granted to private owners.

It is the view of this author that developed-country models cannot wholly be applied to developing countries in which the media systems are too small and underresourced to be considered fully independent and free, especially when the state is the largest advertiser. Further, an adjustment needs to be made to the liberal model created by Hallin and Mancini (2004), while at the same time, there is a need to incorporate elements of the social-responsibility model developed by Siebert, Peterson and Schramm (1956). In this regard, I am making a case for recognition of an emerging liberal-democratic model of media and politics, which has the capacity to evolve into a full liberal-democratic model, but with a healthy sense of social responsibility, taking into account the relative youth of the society in recognition of the fact that democracy involves a process of growth, including the evolution and mutual strengthening of key institutions, while also recognizing that it is largely democratic and liberal, but still emerging, and that therefore, finding its foothold is vital. Such a model is reflective of fundamental realities: Trinidad and Tobago is a small, developing, postcolonial and multiethnic society grounded in democratic traditions but still in transition, forging its way to a stronger democracy within the context of a democratic deficit in the strength of national institutions, as well as in a civic capacity, that attends most societies at this stage of development.

To achieve the status of being classified as a liberal-democratic model of media and politics, a country like Trinidad and Tobago must tread carefully, balancing boldness with the need to recognize the fragility inherent in such societies. The evidence is clear that the media have been able to function well in the early independence period, enjoying some freedom from 1986 to the present, when the system was deregulated. Nevertheless, the media on their own have shown restraint (as in the case of their reportage on the volatile issue of race in the elections and on the issue of internal party conflicts) and have demonstrated a sense of social responsibility, thus carving out a developmental role for the media in the democratic process (a role not necessarily influenced by government but, rather, by self-imposed restraint and self-censorship). This approach should perhaps be more self-consciously pursued, as an emerging democratic model evolves under conditions of freedom and mutually respectful engagement. Such a proposition for an emerging liberal-democratic model has an element of freshness and may well work for other Caribbean and, possibly, other developing countries that have a genuine commitment to democracy.

Conclusion

During the decade under review, all three newspapers, the *Guardian*, *Express* and *Newsday*, demonstrated considerable objectivity when reporting during political campaigns. In general, they were concerned about the leadership of the country and discussion about governance issues. In contrast, they tried to steer the country away from issues that could destabilize the nation, such as race and personal conflicts. However, they were concerned about finding the right leader to govern the country and tended to favour new parties that challenged the status quo and existing regimes by framing new leaders much more positively than incumbent leaders. When governments did not meet the expectations of the media, they were generally hard on leaders, insisting on honesty, transparency and accountability in managing the country's business. In such cases, they were relentless in their coverage of corruption and scandals, which in many instances was interpreted as bias against governments. In addition, the press did show structural bias towards incumbent governments by relying too heavily on politicians as its main sources of information. As a result, coverage tended to be government-driven, with prime ministers being highly featured in newspapers. Unfortunately, reportage tended to be negative towards most governments, creating what has been described as the incumbency disadvantage.

Evidence points to the growing importance of the media in Trinidad and Tobago's young democracy, with the press moving away from being passive intermediaries of information between politicians and the general public and towards actively mediatizing in the political communication process, and thereby having an increasingly greater influence in the outcome of general elections in Trinidad and Tobago. Against this background, it is important to recognize the watchdog role of the media in holding politicians to account, as well as the tendency to self-imposed restraint and support for the harmonious development of the society.

The media in Trinidad and Tobago continue to evolve, as does the relationship between press and politics. Whatever tendencies the press might show, whatever errors the press might make, it can be fatal for a politician to confront the press. The press may not be able to tell you what to think, but it can focus your attention on certain things, which then become central to one's thought process. This, in turn, done consistently, can frame public perception and can facilitate rejection of information outside that frame. Such a bias may be unintended, but it would nevertheless be real and, consequently, have a deep and abiding effect. This makes the media, especially the press, very powerful in a country such as Trinidad and Tobago, and hence the greatest need for balance lies between the media's watchdog role and their conscious, self-imposed restraint.

Glossary

authoritarianism: The dominance of national politics by mainly a single male political leader of both the governing and opposition parties for lengthy periods. In Trinidad and Tobago, the country had a history of male leadership of both the PNM and the UNC.

balanced: Balanced reporting is defined as aiming for neutrality and requires that reporters both present legitimate spokespersons for the conflicting sides in any significant dispute and provide both sides with the same attention. In the context of this book, it also refers to fairness and neutrality in the way the daily press reports on both the governing party and the opposition during political campaigns, as well as the amount of positive and negative coverage given during elections.

columnist: In the context of this book, someone accepted by newspapers as an authority on certain political issues. Commonly referred to as "political pundits", they are observers of and commentators on politics.

conflict frame: The framing of elections by overly focusing on personal conflicts between members of rival political parties as well as among members of the same party. These conflicts also relate to political leaders and their ability to maintain harmonious relationships with members of their own party as well as the opposition.

editorials: Represent the political identity of the newspapers while seeking also to represent the collective voice of their readers. In Trinidad and Tobago, editorials are written by a number of anonymous sources and generally address current issues, including those relating to politics.

frames: The way social reality is constructed in a predictable and patterned way, so as to shape or alter a person's interpretations and preferences. Framing is defined as selecting and highlighting some facets of events and issues and making decisions so as to promote a particular interpretation or solution.

Framing effects can lead to news slant and biased political coverage, resulting in shifting of political power from one party to the opposition.

governing frame: Relates to unity/accommodations entered into by political parties to win elections, such as the NAR and the PP. The country does not have a history of successful third parties, and as a result, accommodations are mostly entered into by opposition parties with smaller parties to try and win elections.

horse-race frame: In the context of this book, the horse-race frame is mostly concerned with the contest or race between rival political leaders and their parties in the lead-up to the national elections. During the period under review, in which five elections were held in ten years, elections were fought fiercely by both the governing party and opposition party during political campaigns.

issue frame: When journalists focus on and report on issues of national importance that are discussed during political campaigns, such as crime, poverty, education, corruption, scandals and media bias.

media: In the context of this book, specifically refers to the press, and in particular the three daily newspapers in Trinidad and Tobago: the *Express*, *Newsday* and the *Guardian*. However, in the context of a small media system, as exists in a country with a population of 1.3 million, the statements attributed to the "press" are sometimes generalized to refer to all media.

media bias: A pattern of favouritism that occurs when one candidate or party receives more news coverage and more favourable coverage during an extended period of time when compared with its opponent. Media bias in Trinidad and Tobago specifically refers to allegations of biased political coverage in the daily newspapers by politicians during elections.

mediatization: Describes the extent to which multimedia messaging has become a central feature of political campaign strategy. Politics is managed by professional campaigners, marketing consultants, public-relations experts, advertisers and pollsters who determine the message and events during political campaigns. Within this context, the role of the press in the context of a general mediatization of campaigns becomes fundamentally important. Mediatization theory argues it is the media that shape and frame the processes and discourse of political communication, as well as the society in which that communication takes place.

objective reporting: Reporting of news without commenting on it, slanting it or shaping its formulation in any way. Objectivity allows journalists to separate facts from values and to report only the facts, and to describe reality as accurately as possible.

political parallelism: The degree to which the structure of the media system parallels that of a party system, as evidenced when certain news organizations are aligned with certain political parties, whose views are represented in their media content or through personal connections.

partisan bias: Level of favouritism given to certain political parties and candidates by media practitioners, including journalists and editors from the *Express, Guardian* and *Newsday,* as well as the alignment of those newspapers with the ideology of the main political parties.

personality frame: The focus of the press on the main political personalities or leaders in both the governing and opposition parties. The personalities involved in the elections take precedence over all other frames during elections in Trinidad and Tobago, and as the contest becomes fiercer, the framing of personalities become more prevalent.

presidentialization: Role of political leaders in shaping the conduct and outcome of elections, with a heavy focus on the appearance and personality of leaders.

press: Newspapers in Trinidad and Tobago, specifically, the three dailies: the *Guardian, Express* and *Newsday.* In the context of this book, the term has been used synonymously with "media".

professionalization: The practice of journalism based on systematic knowledge or doctrine acquired through formal training and education.

structural bias: Norms of journalism or reporter behaviour that favour news about some topics over others, which give some candidates advantages over others.

References

Abbott, J.P. 2011. "Electoral Authoritarianism and the Print Media in Malaysia: Measuring Political Bias and Analyzing Its Cause". *Asian Affairs: An American Review* 38 (1): 1–38.

ANSA McAL Psychological Research Centre. 2010. *Survey of Media Bias*. St Augustine, Trinidad and Tobago: ANSA McAL Psychological Research Centre, University of the West Indies.

Attorney General's Office of Trinidad and Tobago. 1997. *Reform of Media Law: Towards a Free and Responsible Media*. Port of Spain: Government of Trinidad and Tobago.

Barber, M. 2008. "Getting the Picture: Airtime and Lineup Bias on Canadian Networks during the 2006 Federal Election". *Canadian Journal of Communication* 33: 621–37.

Barrow-Giles, C., and T.S.D. Joseph. 2006. *General Elections and Voting in the English-Speaking Caribbean 1992–2005*. Kingston: Ian Randle.

Bennett, W.L., and R.M. Entman. 2001. *Mediated Politics: Communication in the Future of Democracy*. New York: Cambridge University Press.

Brader, T. 2006. *Campaigns for Hearts and Minds: How Emotional Appeals in Political Ads Work*. Chicago: University of Chicago Press.

Broadcasting Commission of Jamaica. 2014. *Broadcasting Law, Regulations and Codes*. Kingston: Jamaica Printing Services.

Cappella, J.N., and K.H. Jamieson. 1997. *Spiral of Cynicism: The Press and the Public Good*. New York: Oxford University Press.

Cenite, M., C. Shing Yee, H. Teck Juan, L. Li Qin and T. Xian Lin. 2008. "Perpetual Development Journalism: Balance and Framing in the 2006 Singapore Election Coverage". *Asian Journal of Communication* 18 (3): 280–95.

Cohen, B.C. 1983. *The Public's Impact on Foreign Policy*. Lanham, MD: University Press of America.

Cruikshand, C.D. 2005. "Trying to Go It Alone and Failing in an Authoritarian Developing State: A Case Study of the *Independent* in Trinidad". Master's thesis, University of Florida.

Curran, J. 1991. "Mass Media and Democracy: A Reappraisal". In *Mass Media and Society*, edited by J. Curran and M. Gurevitch, 82–117. London: Arnold.

De Vreese, C. 2005. "News Framing: Theory and Typology". *Information Design Journal* 13 (1): 51–62.

Druckman, J.N., and M. Parkin. 2005. "The Impact of Media Bias: How Editorial Slant Affects Voters". *Journal of Politics* 67 (4): 1030–49.

Editors' Code of Practice Committee. 1990. "Editors' Code of Practice". https://www.ipso.co.uk/editors-code-of-practice/.

Emmanuel, P.A.M. 1992. *Elections and Party Systems in the Commonwealth Caribbean 1944–1991*. Bridgetown, Barbados: Caribbean Development Research Services.

Entman, R.M. 1989. *Democracy without Citizens: Media and the Decay of American Politics*. New York: Oxford University Press.

Entman, R.M. 1991. "Framing U.S. Coverage of International News: Contrasts in Narratives of the KAL and Iran Air Incidents". *Journal of Communication* 41 (4): 6–27.

———. 2004. *Projections of Power: Framing News, Public Opinion and US Foreign Policy*. Chicago: University of Chicago Press.

———. 2010. "Media Framing Biases and Political Power: Explaining Slant in News of Campaign 2008". *Journalism* 11 (4): 389–408.

Garyantes, D. 2006. "Coverage of the Iraqi Elections: A Textual Analysis of Al-Jazeera and the *New York Times*". Paper presented at the annual meeting for the International Communication Association, Dresden, Germany, 16 June.

Goffman, E. 1974. *Frame Analysis: An Essay on the Organization of Experience*. Boston: Northeastern University Press.

Gordon, K. 1999. *Getting It Write*. Jamaica: Ian Randle.

Grant, L., Gibbings, W. 2009. *An Election Handbook for the Caribbean*: Trinidad and Tobago.

Gulati, G.J. 2004. *News Coverage of Political Campaigns*. New York: Lawrence Erlbaum.

Guyana Elections Commission. 2016. "A Media Code of Conduct". *GECOM: Guyana Elections Commission*. http://www.gecom.org.gy/media_code_of_conduct.html.

Guyana National Broadcasting Commission. 2011. *Act No.17. Broadcasting Act 2011*. Georgetown: Guyana National Printeries Limited.

Hallin, C.D., and P. Mancini. 2004. *Comparing Media Systems: Three Models of Media and Politics*. Cambridge: Cambridge University Press.

Hayes, D. 2008. "Party Reputations, Journalistic Expectations: How Issue Ownership Influences Election News". *Political Communication* 25 (4): 377–400.

IAPA (Inter American Press Association). 1994. "Chapultepec Declaration". *Sociedad Interamericana de Prensa*. http://www.sipiapa.org/contenidos/acerca-de-la-declaracion.html.

House of Representatives. 2010. Trinidad and Tobago Parliament. *Interception of Communications Act 2010*. Port of Spain: Government Printery.

John, G.R. 2002. *Beyond the Front Page: Memoirs of a Caribbean Journalist*. St Augustine, Trinidad and Tobago: School of Continuing Studies, University of the West Indies.

Kahn, K.F., and P.J. Kenney. 2002. "The Slant of the News: How Editorial Endorsements Influence Campaign Coverage and Citizens' views of Candidates". *American Political Science Review* 96 (2): 381–94.

Kenney, K., and C. Simpson. 1993. "Was Coverage of the 1988 Presidential Race by Washington's Two Major Dailies Biased?" *Journalism Quarterly* 70 (2): 345–55.

Kenski, H.C., and K.M. Kenski. 2005. "Explaining the Vote in a Divided Country: The Presidential Election of 2004". In *The 2004 Presidential Campaign: A Communicative Perspective*, edited by R. E. Danton, 301–42. Lanham, MD: Rowan and Littlefield.

Lang, G.E., and K. Lang. 1981. "Watergate: An Exploration of the Agenda-Building Process". In *Agenda Setting: Readings on Media, Public Opinion, Policymaking*, edited by D.L. Protess, E. Maxwell and E. McCombs, 277–89. St Paul, MN: West.

Lilleker, D.G. 2006. *Key Concepts in Political Communication*. London: Sage.

Mazzoleni, G. 2004. "With the Media, without the Media: Reasons and Implications of the Electoral Success of Silvio Berlusconi in 2001". In *European Culture and the Media*, edited by I.B. Bondebjerg and P. Golding, 257–66. Bristol: Intellect.

McChesney, R.W. 1998. "Media Convergence and Globalization". In *Electronic Empires and Local Resistance*, edited by D. Thussu, 27–46. London: Arnold.

McCombs, M. 2004. *Setting the Agenda: The Mass Media and Public Opinion*. London: Polity.

McCombs, M.E., and D.L. Shaw. 1972. "The Agenda Setting Function of the Mass Media". *Public Opinion Quarterly* 36 (2): 176–87.

McQuail, D. 2005. *Communication Theory*. London: Sage.

——. 2008. *McQuail's Mass Communication Theory*. London: Sage.

Media Association of Trinidad and Tobago. 2006. http://mediatrinbago.wordpress.com.

Media Complaints Council. 2009. MCC's Purpose and History. http://www.ttpba.org .tt/general/mccs_purpose_and-history.php.

MORI Caribbean. 2009. "A Report on Opinion Leaders' Panel 2009: Wave 13 Report – A Research Study Conducted for the Government of Trinidad and Tobago".

One Caribbean Media Limited. 2009. "Further Comments and Recommendations on the Revised Draft National Broadcasting Code". Port of Spain.

Patterson, T.E. 1993. *Out of Order*. New York: Vintage.

Petrocik, J.R. 1996. "Issue Ownership in Presidential Elections, with a 1980 Case Study". *American Journal of Political Science* 40 (3): 825–50.

Price, V.D., D. Tewksbury and E. Powers. 1997. "Switching Trains of Thought: The Impact of News Frames on Readers' Cognitive Responses". *Communication Research* 24 (5): 481–508.

Ramcharitar, R. 2005. *Breaking the News: Media and Culture in Trinidad*. Port of Spain: Lexicon.

Reporters Without Borders. 2012. "World Press Freedom Index 2011-2012". https://rsf.org/en/news/press-freedom-index-20112012.

Rhodes, L., and P. Henry. 1995. "State and Media in the English-Speaking Caribbean: The Case of Antigua". *Journalism and Mass Communication Quarterly* 72 (3): 654–663.

Ryan, M. 2001. "Journalistic Ethics, Objectivity, Existential Journalism, Standpoint Epistemology, and Public Journalism". *Journal of Mass Media Ethics* 16 (1): 3–22.

Ryan, S. 2009. *Eric Williams: The Myth and the Man*. Kingston: University of the West Indies Press.

Ryan, S., and R. McCree. 1995. *Ethnicity and the Media in Trinidad and Tobago: A Research Report*. St Augustine: University of the West Indies Centre for Ethnic Studies.

Scheufele, A.D. 1999. "Framing as a Theory of Media Effects". *Journal of Communication* 49 (1): 103–22.

Schudson, M. 2001. "The Objectivity Norm in American Journalism". *Journalism* 2 (2): 149–70.

Schudson, M. 2003. *The Sociology of News*. New York: W.W. Norton.

Siebert, F.S., T. Paterson and W. Schramm. 1956. *Four Theories of the Press: The Authoritarian, Libertarian, Social Responsibility and Soviet Communist Concepts of What the Press Should Be or Do*. Champaign: University of Illinois Press.

Strömbäck, J., and F. Esser. 2014. "Mediatization of Politics. Transforming Democracies and Reshaping Politics". In *Mediatization of Communication*, edited by K. Lundby, 375–403. Berlin: De Gruyter Mouton.

Strömbäck, J., and A. Shehata. 2007. "Structural Biases in British and Swedish Election News Coverage". *Journalism Studies* 8 (5): 798–812.

Trinidad and Tobago. 1997. Cabinet Minute No. 1481. "Report of Working Group Appointed by Cabinet to Prepare a National Policy on Telecommunications for Trinidad and Tobago". http://www.tiragreene.com/policy2.htm.

——. Task Force on Telecommunications. 1989. *The Establishment of a Telecommunications Authority for the Republic of Trinidad and Tobago*. Port of Spain: Government Printery.

Takens, J., N. Ruigrok, A. Van Hoof and O.Scholten. 2008. "Leaning to the Right or Leaning to the Left? Dutch Media and Politics". International Communication Association.

Telecommunications Authority of Trinidad and Tobago. 2014. *A Draft Broadcasting Code for the Republic of Trinidad and Tobago*. Port of Spain: Telecommunications Authority of Trinidad and Tobago.

Trent, S.J., and R.V. Friedenberg. 2008. *Political Campaign Communication: Principles and Practices*. Lanham, MD: Roman and Littlefield Publishers, Inc.

Trinidad and Tobago Publishers and Broadcasters Association. 2009. Media Complaints Council. http://wwwttpba.org.tt

Waisbord, S. 2002. "Grandes Gigantes: Media Concentration in Latin America". *openDemocracy*. https://www.opendemocracy.net/media-globalmediaownership/article_64.jsp.

Voltmer, K. 2007. *Mass Media and Political Communication in New Democracies*. London: Routledge.

Wang, X. 2003. "Media Ownership and Objectivity". Master's thesis, Louisiana State University.

Wesley, J.J., and M. Colborne. 2005. "Framing Democracy: Media Politics and the 2004 Alberta Election". Paper presented at the annual meeting of the Canadian Political Science Association, London, Ontario.

Westerstahl, J. 1983. "Objective News Reporting: General Premises". *Communication Research* 10 (3): 403–24.

Wong, K. 2004. "Asian-Based Development Journalism and Political Elections: Press Coverage of the 1999 General Elections in Malaysia". *International Communication Gazette* 66 (1): 25–40.

Zeldes, G.A., F. Fico, S. Carpenter and A. Diddi. 2008. "Partisan Balance and Bias in Network Coverage of the 2000 and 2004 Presidential Elections". *Journal of Broadcasting and Electronic Media* 52 (4): 563–80.

Index

www.ingramcontent.com/pod-product-compliance
Lightning Source LLC
Chambersburg PA
CBHW030652270326
41929CB00007B/323